PLUMBING AND WIRING

To Tommy
from Mum
with love
Xmas. 1988

TIME
LIFE
BOOKS

This volume is part of a series offering home owners detailed instructions on repairs, construction and improvements which they can undertake themselves.

HOME REPAIR
AND IMPROVEMENT

PLUMBING
AND WIRING

BY THE EDITORS OF
TIME-LIFE BOOKS

TIME-LIFE BOOKS
AMSTERDAM

TIME-LIFE BOOKS
EUROPEAN EDITOR: Kit van Tulleken
Design Director: Ed Skyner
Photography Director: Pamela Marke
Chief of Research: Vanessa Kramer
Chief Sub-Editor: Ilse Gray

HOME REPAIR AND IMPROVEMENT
EDITORIAL STAFF FOR PLUMBING AND WIRING
Project Director: Jackie Matthews
Editors: Tony Allan, Christopher Farman, Nicoletta
Flessati, Gillian Moore
Writer: Deborah Thompson
Researchers: Eleanor Lines, Elizabeth Loving
Designers: Rick Bowring, Paul Reeves
Sub-Editors: Charles Boyle, Sally Rowland

EDITORIAL PRODUCTION
Chief: Ellen Brush
Production Assistants: Stephanie Lee,
Jane Lillicrap
Editorial Department: Theresa John, Debra Lelliott

THE CONSULTANTS: Richard Pilling, the chief consultant for the
plumbing chapters, is a lecturer in Plumbing and Mechanical
Services at Erith College of Technology, Belvedere, Kent. He has
also worked as a heating engineer in industry.

John P. Cutting is Assistant Director (Technical) of the Electrical
Contractors' Association. He has been an electrical consultant to
industry for over 35 years, and with David Haviland (below) is
involved in the preparation of new safety standards and regulations.

David J. Haviland, Senior Engineer at the Electrical Contractors'
Association, is an adviser to local authorities. He has been
responsible for the design and installation of electrical systems in
schools, hospitals and other public building projects.

Contents

1

New Scope for the Home Plumber

Pipes in your home. The network of piping on the left includes the three main types—waste, vent and supply—of a plumbing system. The thickest *(second from left)* is a main soil and waste stack, channelling wastes into the sewer or septic tank; a subsidiary waste pipe *(lower right)* empties into the main stack. To keep air moving through the waste pipes and to eliminate sewer gases, vent pipes *(far left)* may be necessary, especially in large buildings such as blocks of flats, to connect the waste system to a roof opening; in most household systems, the vent consists simply of an extension of the soil stack itself to roof level. Thin vertical and horizontal pipes of smaller diameter take the hot and cold water supply to outlets around the house; the wheel-headed gate-valves can shut off the flow when fixtures need maintenance or repair.

Most people fix dripping taps as a matter of routine. Beyond that chore, plumbing generally has been left to plumbers. Yet today a whole list of tasks once the province of professionals—replacing old fixtures and taps with modern, easier-to-use types, extending pipes to add or relocate equipment, installing a washing machine or a garden tap—can be and often must be handled by amateurs. Economy is one reason; professionals usually charge so much for their time that a householder may save a considerable amount of money completing a job himself, even if this necessitates buying a special tool that will be used only once. Perhaps more important is the revolution in plumbing techniques that has eliminated the requirements for brute strength and dexterous skills; new materials are light in weight and many are assembled simply by tightening nuts or applying glue. And an increasingly significant factor in the trend to do-it-yourself plumbing is the growing concern for a resource long taken for granted. Water supplies are under constantly increasing demand, and care and economy in the use of water in private plumbing systems has become essential.

Every family can keep its water consumption down—while enjoying the many conveniences of new equipment—by a regular programme of repairs and a carefully planned choice of minor alterations.

☐ Repairing a dripping tap *(pages 28–31)* while it is still in the drop-by-drop stage saves an amazing quantity of water—a slow trickle wastes a bathful of water a day, and a steady stream wastes enough water to meet all the family's daily needs.

☐ Repairing a faulty float valve in a W.C. cistern *(pages 42–44)* will prevent an incessant overflow that can be irritating to hear as well as extremely wasteful of water.

☐ Replacing an old W.C. cistern *(pages 76–79)* with a new pan and a cistern designed to save water can reduce water consumption by many litres a day. The double-flushing type makes it possible to choose whether to use all or only half of the water in the cistern.

☐ If you fit a shower *(pages 68–73)*, you can use a fraction of the hot water required for a bath, giving savings both in water consumption and in the fuel required for heating.

Using the right tools and methods, you can meet the crises and increase the conveniences of your plumbing system—seal a burst pipe or thaw a frozen one *(pages 14–17)*, even unclog a blocked main drain *(page 23)*. The modern plumbing materials and fittings that have made these tasks simpler have been largely standardized; the pipes, fittings and fixtures described in this book are available almost everywhere in the British Isles. Some varieties of copper piping and the increasingly popular plastic pipe are semi-rigid, and easier to manipulate and install than traditional materials such as steel and cast iron. To attach a connection to these pipes, you may not need even to solder or glue a fitting: in many situations the job is easily and efficiently done by a compression-type fitting *(page 55)* that simply screws together.

You will be able to use these new repair and modernization methods with confidence if you understand how the plumbing system operates. The fundamental principles of physical science govern the behaviour of the water in the pipes, but most of the facts that you need to know are very simple. In a home plumbing system, cold water from the public supply flows into the house under pressure through a service pipe. Inside the house, the cold water taps may be supplied either direct from the mains by a network of pipes, or indirectly from a cold water storage cistern in the attic or loft that is kept topped up from the mains (pages 12–13). The hot water cylinder that feeds water through a separate pipe system to the hot taps is almost invariably supplied from the cold water storage cistern in the house.

While the supply system brings water into the house under pressure, the drainage system that carries off waste water and sewage operates by the force of gravity. Waste pipes always slant downwards or run vertically, and bends are gentle to reduce restrictions to the flow. The central element in the drainage system, comparable to the main service pipe of the supply system, is the large vertical pipe called the soil stack. In some houses there is both a soil stack to remove sewage and a separate waste stack for other household waste water, but in most modern installations a single stack collects all the wastes. Whichever system is used, however, all the household wastes and sewage are channelled into a sloping drain that carries them out into the public sewer (normally under the street) or, if the house is not connected to mains drainage, into a septic tank.

To prevent foul air from making its way back up the soil and waste pipes and entering the living space in and around the building, every appliance and some waste pipes empty into traps—U-shaped passages permanently filled with water that serve as barriers against sewer gases. Sink and basin traps are generally accessible and easy to clear or, if necessary, to replace (pages 38–39); baths and showers can be cleared in the same way, but access to the traps may be more difficult if you want to replace them.

The free passage of air throughout the drainage system is essential to maintain atmospheric pressure equally at every point. Otherwise, any reduction of pressure below the seal in a trap will allow the higher atmospheric pressure above it to push the water out of the trap, destroying the seal and allowing sewer gases to enter the room. Atmospheric pressure in the main soil and waste stacks is maintained by an open vent at its top—a chimney-like pipe rising through the roof that allows air to pass freely in and out. Because sewer gases can and do rise back up this vent, the pipe must open well above the level on which the people in the house are living.

Alterations of any kind in your plumbing system are controlled by regulations issued by your local authority. The regulations have the force of law and must be observed, but they do not usually prevent you from working on your own plumbing system, so long as you follow their requirements. The by-laws covered by those parts of the Public Health Act dealing with drains and sewers control all interference with public and private sewerage, so you should always obtain the advice of the local authority before embarking on such work. Because they are established to meet the special problems of the particular area in which you live, observing the regulations is not only necessary, but is also a wise precaution for your own health and safety.

Depending on the soil through which the water percolates before reaching you, your water may be hard or soft—that is, relatively rich or poor in dissolved minerals. In turn, the nature of your water may sometimes affect the kind of materials you should use. In some areas, for example, where the water is extremely acidic, brass fittings are prohibited because, by a process known as dezincification, the acidic water dissolves out the zinc from the brass (a copper and zinc alloy), eventually destroying the fitting and causing leaks. In these districts, gunmetal or solid copper fittings must be substituted for brass. Water may also be so acidic that it can dissolve lead or copper. Normally the local authority's water treatment regulates this acidity by a method known as Ph correction, but in some areas it may not. If you are in any doubt about the nature of your water supply, consult your local water authority before selecting materials.

It is a general requirement of the Institution of Electrical Engineers wiring regulations that unless a metal pipe is effectively connected to the main bonding system of a house *(page 96)*, it must be bonded to a fixed electrical appliance where there is a possibility of the two being touched simultaneously. It is important, therefore, that you establish whether or not the metal pipes in your house are part of the earth-bonding system before you begin any work on them. Modern housing will have a schedule of the plumbing and wiring which will map the bonding route. Older housing may also have had a bonding system installed during re-wiring, but it is doubtful that there will be any accompanying schedule. If you intend to replace a section of metal pipe that is part of the bonding system with plastic, you must provide an alternative link. Call in an electrician. If you are simply replacing one metal section with another, use a temporary bond—an earth continuity wire, available at good D.I.Y. shops—clamped to either side of the point where the break will be made. For absolute safety whilst working on earth-bonded pipes, switch off the mains electricity supply.

By-laws and regulations are available at the public library or the offices of your local authority. If you plan extensive work it is helpful to have a copy of your own. You will not need it for ordinary repair or replacement, but in a new installation it is a useful guide to the right plumbing practices and materials for your area.

Tool Kit
for Plumbing

With only a few specialized tools you can be ready not only to meet most plumbing emergencies, but also to install and replace pipes and appliances.

For unclogging wastes you will need a rubber force cup or plunger. A drain auger draws out blockages from sink and bath wastes; for W.C.s, use a cleaning rod or a specially designed W.C. auger housed in a cylinder that positions the end of the wire coil accurately to enter the trap.

To loosen and tighten joints and appliances, adjustable spanners and pliers are basic equipment. In addition, several types of wrench are helpful. The choice depends partly on personal preference and partly on convenience and accessibility for a particular job. A basin wrench is designed to tighten nuts behind sinks and in other enclosed spaces. A toothed pipe wrench holds the curved surface of tubing in a firm grip, but it can damage softer materials such as copper or plastic; if necessary, when using one, you can muffle the teeth by wrapping a cloth round them. Use a smooth-jawed tool for nuts and fittings with plane faces.

To fix leaks caused by worn valve seats, you need a tap-reseating tool with assorted cutting discs and guides to grind smooth the damaged face.

For cutting and joining copper pipe, use a pipe cutter with a built-in reamer for scraping off burrs inside the cut edge. A coiled pipe-bending spring helps you bend pipe without kinks. To join sections of copper pipe by capillary soldering, you need steel wool, a wire brush for cleaning inside pipe ends, flux and a brush to apply it, solder and a fireproof mat to protect inflammable materials nearby. A liquid petroleum gas torch—butane (shown here) or propane—supplies the necessary heat. To make a watertight seal at a screw-thread connection, use PTFE tape (short for poly-tetra-fluor-ethylene).

For some jobs you may want to hire additional tools, such as a steel drift for flaring copper pipe ends *(page 56)*, or a link pipe cutter for cutting cast-iron pipes *(page 62)*. Working with plastic pipe calls for only solvent cement *(page 59)*.

FIREPROOF MAT

WIRE BRUSH

FLUX APPLICATOR

PTFE TAPE

SOLDER

FLUX

STEEL WOOL

PIPE-BENDING SPRING

PIPE CUTTER

BUTANE TORCH

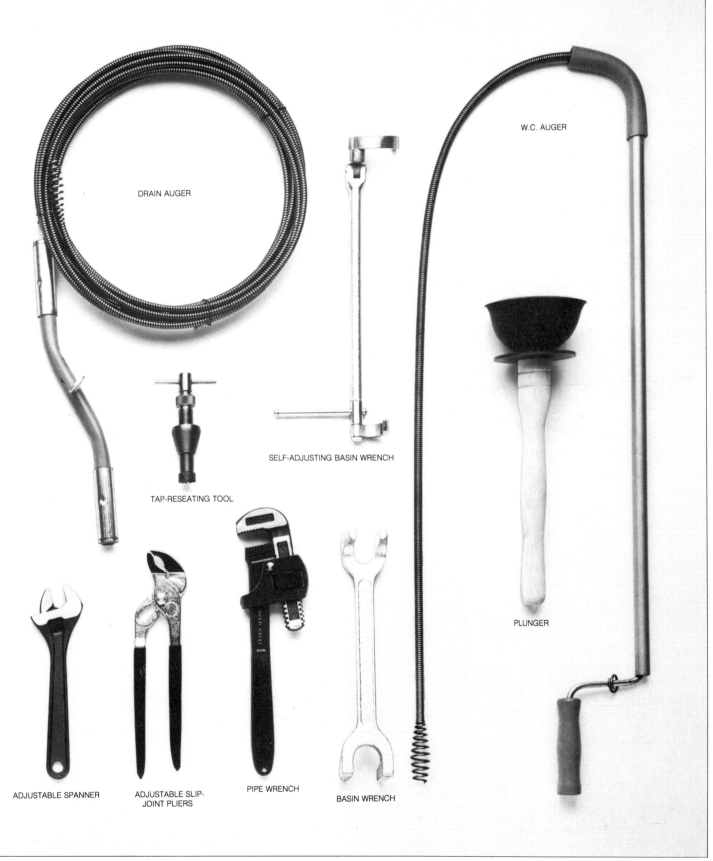

DRAIN AUGER

W.C. AUGER

SELF-ADJUSTING BASIN WRENCH

TAP-RESEATING TOOL

PLUNGER

ADJUSTABLE SPANNER

ADJUSTABLE SLIP-
JOINT PLIERS

PIPE WRENCH

BASIN WRENCH

What Goes On Inside the Pipes

The diagrams on these pages show typical household pipe systems for the two principal forms of water supply and drainage found in the United Kingdom. Both supply systems illustrated may be found with either one of the drainage systems. (Pipes for central heating, which is beyond the scope of this book, are not shown.) The details of the piping will vary from house to house according to the location of appliances, but the main features are constant. Track the layout of the pipes in your own home before you attempt any repairs or alterations.

The supply system may be either direct or indirect. In the direct type (below), the mains water is conducted through the vertical pipe known as the rising main straight to the cold taps and appliances throughout the house; in the indirect system (opposite page), the rising main fills a cold water storage cistern located above the hot water cylinder—usually in the roof space—and water is then drawn from the cistern to supply the needs of the household. In this scheme, the law requires that one tap (usually in the kitchen) should always be supplied direct from the mains, so that the occupants can drink water that has not been exposed to airborne bacteria

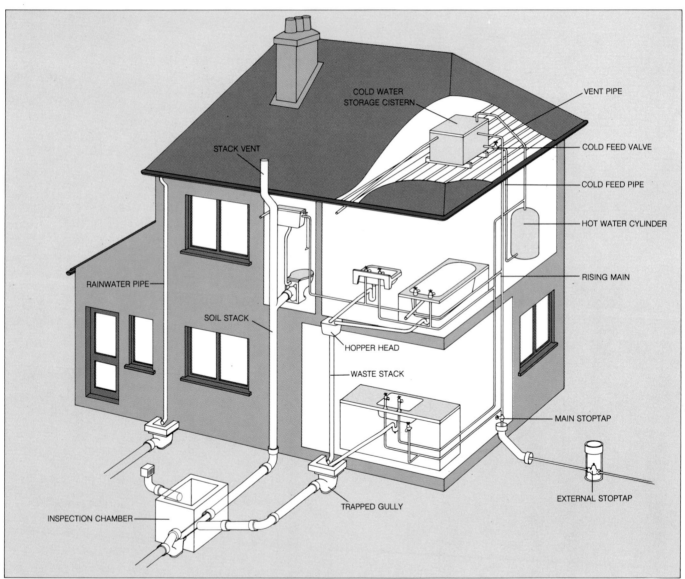

The direct system. In a direct supply system, the cold water storage cistern feeds only the hot water cylinder, while all the cold taps, W.C. cisterns and other appliances are supplied under mains pressure. The double-stack drainage system, common in older houses, has a soil stack carrying sewage and a separate waste stack for other household wastes, both positioned against the external wall of the house. They are usually constructed of cast iron, but many have been replaced by PVC at some time when they needed repair. The waste stack is shown here with an open hopper head, but it could also be a sealed pipe, vented at roof level, like the soil stack.

while stored in the cistern. A second mains tap is permitted but not required; all others must be drawn from the cistern.

The service pipe by which the water supply enters the house from the public water main is controlled by a stoptap designed to act also as a non-return valve. This is a precaution against the accident of back-siphonage, whereby an unexpected drop in mains pressure might, in unusual circumstances, allow contaminated water from an appliance within the house to be siphoned back into the mains, where it could pollute the supply. If the stoptap is outside the boundary of the property, it belongs to the water authority; if inside, it is the householder's responsibility.

Just inside the house is usually another stoptap, with which the owner can interrupt the flow into the household system, for instance before dealing with a leak. It is useful to have stoptaps and valves at other points in the system as well, so that you can isolate and drain different sections of piping when you want to work on them.

The drainage system may be either the single-stack type *(below)*, in which W.C.s and all other appliances empty into the same soil and waste stack, or double-stack *(opposite page)*, where the soil stack for sewage is separate from the waste stack for water from baths, basins and sinks. All soil stacks, whether separate or combined, have a vent above roof level, to keep air flowing through the system. So that the sewers will not be overburdened by sudden storms, surface water—rain—sometimes flows through gutters and a trapped gully into a separate drain.

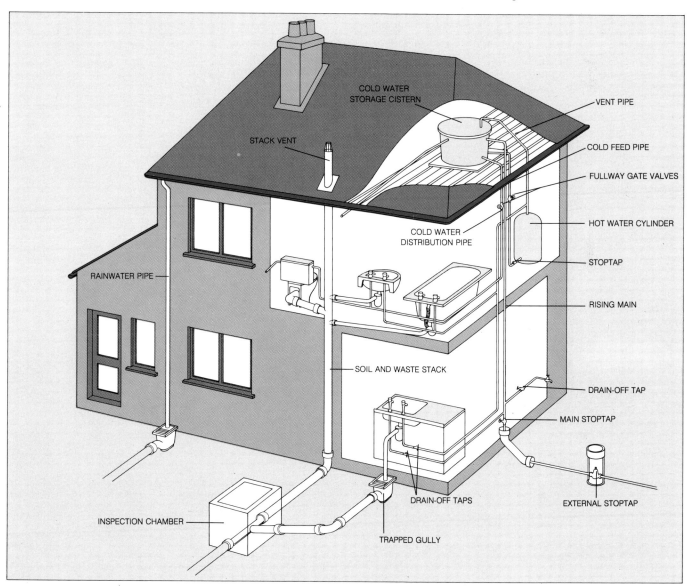

The indirect system. In a typical indirect supply system, only the kitchen cold tap and a garden tap are connected direct to the mains. The remaining taps and appliances, and the hot water cylinder, are fed from the cold water storage cistern. The single combined soil and waste stack, normally built of PVC piping, is located inside the house. The water from the kitchen sink is shown discharging into its own trapped gully; however, it might equally well feed into the main stack like the rest of the appliances in the house.

Shutting Down the Plumbing System

At one time or another, you may need to put all the fixtures, appliances, taps and pipes in your plumbing system out of operation. When you do major repairs or installations that call for cutting into the main pipes, you must both shut off the incoming water and drain out the existing supply before you can start work. If you leave a house empty and unheated for the winter, you must also weatherproof the system to protect it from bursting in freezing temperatures. Whatever the occasion, be sure to reserve several litres of water for drinking or cooking before you shut off the supply.

In order to drain your system efficiently, follow this check list:

☐ Cut off the house water supply by closing the main stoptap.

☐ Turn off the gas or electricity to the boiler and any water-heating appliances.

☐ If you have hot-water central heating, open the drain tap, located either on the boiler or adjacent pipework, to empty the system. A hosepipe is usually necessary to direct the water to an outside drain. Next, open all the radiator valves. Then remove an air vent from a radiator on the top floor so that air will replace the water as it drains down. (In the case of indirect water supply systems, it is not necessary to drain the central heating if you are merely carrying out repairs or alterations to the basic supply and drainage piping in your house, since the central heating operates on a separate circuit.)

☐ Working floor by floor, starting at the top, open all hot and cold water taps including all baths, showers and outdoor taps—and flush all W.C.s.

☐ Open the drain taps on the water heater and the water treatment equipment, if you have any in the house.

☐ Finally, open the drain taps on the main supply line in order to release any water that may still remain in the pipes.

At this stage, your plumbing system will be adequately drained for repair or remodelling work. If you are closing the house for the winter, it is a good idea to take additional precautions. Walk through the house to check that wherever water can collect is drained.

For cold weather protection, simply add a tablespoon of glycerine to the water remaining in fixture and W.C. traps; alternatively, pour in some kitchen salt. Either measure will keep the water from freezing and possibly bursting the traps, while still allowing it to function as a barrier against sewer gases.

When spring comes or after the repair is completed, you will have to refill your system. First, close the drain tap on the main water supply pipe. Close all the taps throughout the house, including those on the boiler, hot water heater and any water treatment equipment. If you have hot water heating, replace the air vent on the radiator from which it was removed. Then open the main stoptap slowly to bring fresh water into the system. The radiators must be air-vented and filled before you light the boiler. Check that the ball valves shut off properly; this is particularly important when the system has been shut down for a time. Finally, turn on the gas or electricity supply to the boiler and hot water heater and follow the relighting procedure that you will find specified on gas-fired equipment.

Taps will splutter when you first use them because of air trapped in the pipes, but this condition will soon correct itself.

First Aid for Frozen Pipes

The pipes in a properly constructed and heated house are safe from freezing even during the most severe cold spell. If, however, the heating system breaks down, or an empty house is left unheated, the indoor temperature will plummet, and you must act quickly to keep pipes from freezing and bursting *(below)*. Even in an otherwise well-built house, pipes that run through an unprotected basement or garage can freeze during very cold weather.

If pipes do freeze, the first sign may be a tap that refuses to yield water. But all too often the damage is announced by a flood from a leak after the ice has thawed. Water expands in volume by 10 per cent as it begins to freeze, generating pressure that splits pipes, especially where expansion is impeded by joints or bends. Ice may form throughout a long, straight section before it meets an obstruction and cracks the pipe, so the entire length of pipe that supplies a stopped tap should be considered suspect. If you have non-manipulative compression joints *(page 55)*, check them to see if expanding ice has pushed the pipe ends free of the joints.

When you prepare to thaw a section of pipe, keep the affected tap open to let water vapour and melting ice run out. Once you have marked the leaks for repair *(pages 16–17)*, turn off the water supply. Apply temporary patches, then partially open the main stoptap; the movement of water through the frozen section will aid the thawing process. Guard the surrounding area against water damage *(box, page 17)*, in case other leaks have gone undetected.

There are several precautions you can take to prevent pipes from freezing. In an unheated house, the only infallible way is to drain the plumbing system, as described opposite; but in other circumstances you can choose from several methods.

☐ If power is available, plug in an electric heater or heat lamp, or hang a 100 watt bulb near vulnerable pipes.

☐ Keep a door ajar between a heated room and an unheated room with pipes.

☐ Insulate exposed pipes with the wrap-on or snap-on varieties of lagging available commercially, or temporarily wrap several layers of newpaper loosely round the pipes and tie with string.

☐ If the temperature drops suddenly and you have no time to install insulation, you could turn on the taps for brief periods. Any water in exposed pipes that may be about to freeze will thus be replaced by water at a higher temperature.

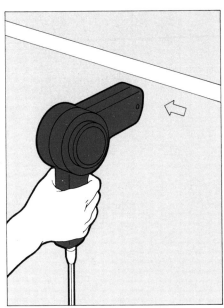

Hair drier. If you have electricity, an appliance that blows warm air, such as a hair drier or a tank-type vacuum cleaner with the hose set into the outlet end, can be used to thaw a frozen pipe. Apply heat near the open tap first, then work gradually back along the pipe. If the pipe is made of plastic, be careful not to overheat it.

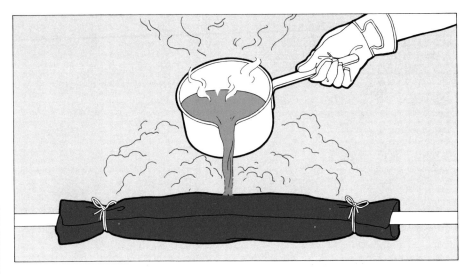

Hot water. If you are thawing a frozen pipe during a power failure in which you still have some means of heating water, tie rags or towels round the frozen section and soak them with boiling water from a kettle or saucepan. Continue pouring a light stream of water over the rags to keep them hot and saturated until the ice in the pipe has melted.

Heat lamp. If the suspected ice blockage is behind a wall or otherwise out of reach, set an electric heat lamp nearby. Keep it at least 150 mm from the wall to avoid scorching paint or wallpaper. For greater flexibility in handling, you can fix the bulb into the socket of a portable work lamp. Pipes that disappear into the ceiling can also be thawed with a heat lamp; hang the lamp directly below the frozen section.

Emergency Pipe Repairs

Pipes have a disconcerting way of springing a leak on Saturday night, after your friendly plumber has gone away for the weekend. Fortunately, some fixes, easy to make using the odds and ends on a workbench, will usually tide you over until you can make (or commission) a permanent repair *(pages 52–63)*.

When you discover a leak in a supply pipe, the first thing to do, of course, is shut off the water supply to the damaged section *(pages 14–15)* so you can proceed to plug the hole.

An application of epoxy glue or plastic tape is the quickest emergency procedure. Various "bandages" or plugs are even better. But before trying any remedy, make sure the pipe surface is dry enough for adhesives or sleeves to hold.

In the case of a leaking supply pipe that is not frozen, completely drain and dry the affected section if possible—an electric hair drier does a quick job. Damaged pipes that are frozen should be left unthawed and undrained until patching is completed. Waste pipes and traps, unlike supply pipes, are not under pressure and normally contain no water (apart from the trap seal) when not in use.

A Patch for a Larger Leak

A hose patch. An effective temporary patch can be made by splitting a section of rubber hose lengthwise so that it will fit round the pipe *(right)*. Strong, flexible wire, such as that used for hanging pictures, will serve to secure the hose—make a series of loops along the patch, spaced about 25 mm apart, and twist each loop tight with a pair of pliers.

A Patch for a Tiny Leak

1 **Plugging a hole with a pencil.** A good emergency plug for a small leak in a supply pipe is a pencil point jammed into the hole and broken off; the soft graphite point will conform to the shape of the opening and seal the leak.

2 **Securing the plug.** Dry the surface of the pipe after the leak has been plugged, then roll heavy tape over the damaged area to hold the plug in place. Wrap the tape several centimetres to the left and the right of the leak.

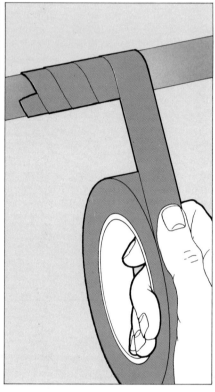

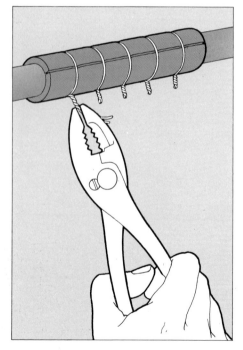

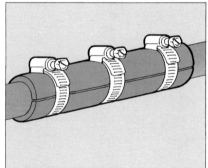

Securing hose with jubilee clips. To fix a hose patch with uniform pressure, use jubilee clips as on a motor car hose *(above)*. These clips can be adjusted to fit virtually any diameter of water pipe. It is best to install at least three clips over the patch.

A Patch of Epoxy Adhesive

Coating and bandaging a split. Epoxy glue makes a useful emergency repair for a cracked pipe. First drain and dry the damaged pipe. Mix the glue—available in kit form from plumbers' merchants—according to the instructions and spread it generously over and around the crack. Bandage the pipe tightly with nylon or fibreglass tape and apply a second layer of adhesive. Leave the patch to dry.

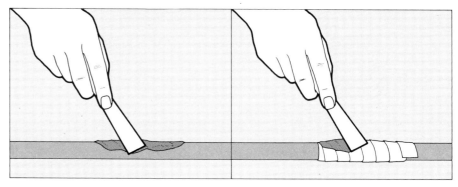

Minimizing Damage if a Leak Floods You Out

Often the first sign of a leaking pipe will be a spreading stain on a wall or ceiling or a puddle on the floor. To prevent further damage, shut off the water supply immediately, before trying to trace the leak and repair it.

You can sometimes anticipate water damage and keep it to a minimum. Where leaking pipes are concealed above the ceiling and a water stain is visible, place a waterproof sheet on the floor and position a catch basin under the wet area. If water is leaking from a ceiling light fitting, shut off the electricity and drain the fixture by removing its cover. Poke a hole through the ceiling or remove a section of it to let any remaining water drain out. Stand out of the way!

During a plumbing freeze-up, take precautions against leaks until you can be certain the pipes have suffered no damage. Since the leaks will be frozen until the pipes thaw, waterproof the suspect area with plastic dustsheets like those used by painters. If you spot a crack, clamp a patch on it *(opposite page)*. And be ready with a few extra bowls and buckets in case undetected leaks reveal themselves.

If you arrive on the scene too late to avert a flood, you can still construct a makeshift dam from sandbags or rolled-up rugs that will prevent the flood from spreading to other rooms. For a bad flood, you may need to use a submersible pump, usually available from tool-hire firms. If the situation is desperate, telephone the local fire brigade, which will always help in an emergency.

Leaks at Joints

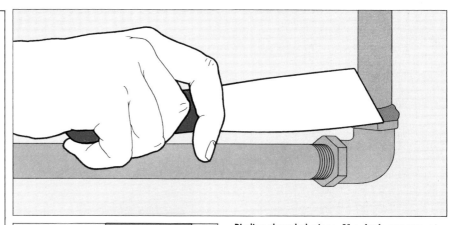

Binding threaded pipes. If a leak appears at a threaded joint, drain the pipe, dry the damaged area and apply epoxy cement over the leaking joint. Allow the epoxy to harden completely, according to the manufacturer's instructions, before restoring water pressure. Epoxy also can be used on plastic joints.

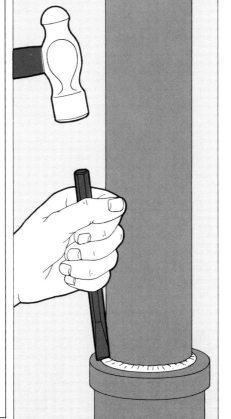

Fixing a lead-caulked joint. If water seeps from a lead-caulked spigot and socket joint, use a hammer and chisel to tamp down the lead inside the socket of the pipe. Since the lead is soft enough to be reshaped over the weak spot, this simple procedure often is sufficient to reseal the joint. Check first, however, that the leak is not due to a crack in the socket. If it is, the pipe will probably need replacing *(pages 62–63)*, since tamping down the lead might simply widen the crack and worsen the leak.

Time-Tested Methods for Unclogging Wastes

A waste blockage may be in the trap under the fixture, in a branch pipe carrying waste from several fixtures, or in the main drain or sewer *(pages 12–13)*.

If only one fixture is blocked or sluggish, start by cleaning its trap. If several fixtures are clogged, follow the techniques shown on the opposite page and pages 20 and 22–23 for cleaning branch drains and main drains. When working with a branch drain or a main drain, remember to warn anyone else in the house not to use any of the appliances that empty into it, or you will have a flood.

An ordinary plunger and a drain auger are not only the easiest unclogging tools to use, but they are also the most effective and the safest. Devices that use compressed air often impact the blockage that you are trying to clear, and they may loosen or blow apart fragile pipes.

It is not advisable to use chemical drain cleaners in a fixture that is completely blocked. The most powerful cleaners contain caustic components that are dangerous and can harm fixtures if left too long in them. If the chemical cleaner does not clear the drain effectively, you will be exposed to the caustic when you open a cleaning eye or remove a trap.

After a drain has been cleaned, chemical cleaners do serve a useful purpose. When they are used regularly—every two weeks or so—they can help to prevent a build-up of debris in a drain that could lead to a future blockage.

Basins and Sinks

1 Using a plunger. If the appliance has an overflow opening, plug it with wet rags. If you have a washing machine or dishwasher that shares a waste pipe with the sink, any air gap provided for the machine must also be plugged. Be sure there is enough water in the basin to cover the plunger cup completely. Coat the rim of the cup evenly with petroleum jelly and centre the cup over the plug hole. Without breaking the seal between the drain and the cup, pump down and up with short, rapid strokes 10 times, then jerk the plunger up from the drain quickly. Repeat the procedure several more times if necessary. If the waste still remains clogged, try Step 2.

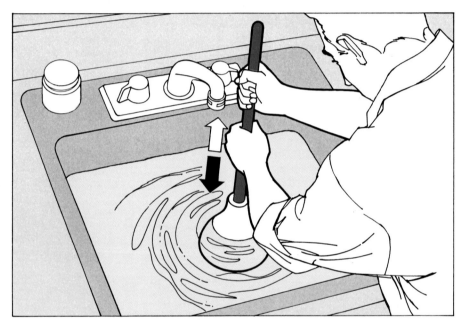

2 Using an auger. If the sink has a strainer in the waste, remove it. Then feed a drain auger into the waste by winding the handle clockwise. As you push the auger wire farther into the drain, alternately loosen and tighten the thumbscrew on the auger handle. When you hook something move the auger backwards and forwards slowly while winding, then withdraw the auger wire slowly while continuing to wind in the same direction. Pour hot water and detergent through the trap to clean away residual grease or oils. If the auger does not clear the trap, try Step 3.

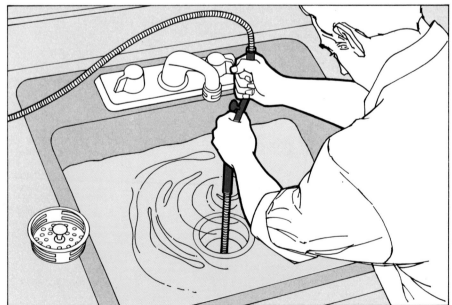

3 **Working through the cleaning eye.** If the trap under the clogged fixture has a cleaning eye, place a bucket under the trap and remove the threaded eye. After water has emptied from the trap and sink, straighten a wire coat hanger, form a small hook in one end, and probe through the trap. If the obstruction is near the opening, you should be able to dislodge it or hook it and draw it out. If not, feed a drain auger first up to the sink opening, then through the back half of the trap. If the blockage is not in the trap, try cleaning beyond the trap as shown on page 20.

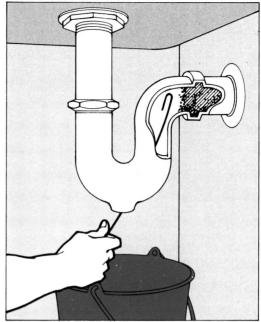

4 **Removing a trap for cleaning.** If the trap has no cleaning eye, shut off the water, unscrew the nut that attaches the trap to the threaded sink waste and detach the trap. Clean it with detergent and a bottle brush *(below)*. To clear a modern bottle trap, unscrew the bottom half of the trap and probe the fixture *(right, below)*. Reassemble the trap and turn on the water. If the drain is still clogged, try the method shown on page 20.

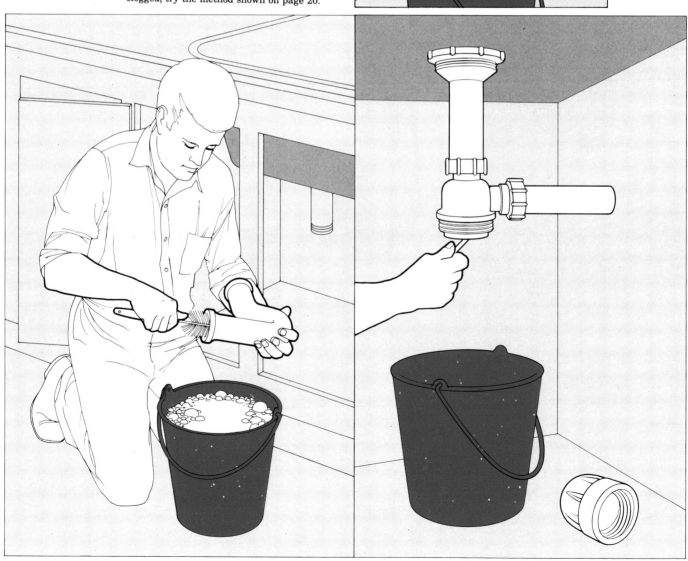

5 **Augering branch drains.** With the trap removed, wind a drain auger into the exposed end of the pipe. The blockage may be in the vertical pipe behind the fixture or in the near-horizontal pipe that connects with the main stack serving the entire house. If the auger goes freely through the waste pipe until it enters the stack, the blockage is probably in a section of the main drainage system, in which case you should clear it by the methods shown on pages 22–23. If your waste pipe is made of push-fit plastic sections *(page 58)* and is readily accessible, you may be able to dismantle it section by section until you reach the blockage, emptying out any water the pipes contain into a bucket as you go.

Unblocking Bath Wastes

The techniques for unblocking bath wastes are the same as for sinks and basins, except that the trap on a bath—hidden away at floor level behind the side panels of the bath—is usually more difficult to reach than that of a sink or basin.

As with sinks and basins, a rubber plunger is the first tool to try. Block up the bath's overflow opening with a damp rag so that the force from the plunger is not dissipated upwards. Use the plunger as a plug and make sure that there is enough water in the bath to cover the cup completely, then pump the plunger vigorously up and down.

If the blockage does not disperse immediately, persevere: the force transmitted from the rubber cup through the water in the pipe may be pushing the obstruction along the waste pipe by degrees, until it breaks down or is freed by being ejected into a main pipe of larger diameter.

If the plunger does not succeed, try a drain auger. The blockage is most likely to be in the trap and it should be possible to remove it by working with the auger through the plughole, according to the instructions in Step 2 on page 18.

If, however, the blockage lies in a branch drain beyond the trap, it may be necessary to remove the trap. To gain access to the trap, you will have to remove a side or end panel from the bath. Bath panels come in many variations, but they generally conform to one of two basic types.

The panel may be made of hardboard or plywood, and held in place near the edges, usually with domed mirror screws. In that case, unscrew and remove the domed tops of the screws by twisting them anticlockwise; underneath you will find the slotted heads of the screws that fix the panel to the bath. These are simply removed with a screwdriver.

Other baths have moulded plastic panels which are flexible enough to be slotted into place under the lip of the bath. Remove such panels by bending them until you can slip the top edge out from its mooring. Then unscrew or dismantle the trap as described on page 19.

Unblocking W.C.s

1 Using a plunger. If a blocked W.C. pan is full to the rim, empty out half its contents. If the pan is empty, add water up to the normal level. Fit a large rubber plunger over the wide opening near the bottom of the pan. Pump 10 times with short, rapid strokes, then lift the plunger quickly. If the blockage has been cleared, you will hear a gurgling sound and the water in the pan will return to its normal level. If the water level sinks slightly but not down to the normal level, the blockage has been only partially removed, in which case you will need to pump again. When you think you have completely cleared the obstruction, test by flushing the W.C.

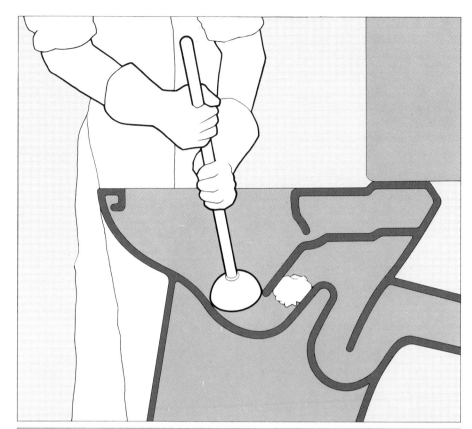

2 Using a W.C. auger. Add or remove water as in Step 1. The W.C. auger—designed specially for clearing W.C.s—has a cranking handle attached to a long sleeve, shaped to guide the auger directly into the trap. Hold the sleeve firmly near the top and wind the hook slowly clockwise into the trap until you reach the obstruction. The auger shown here is being used on a plain washdown W.C. *(right)*; it is also suitable for clearing a close-coupled siphonic suite *(right, above)*.

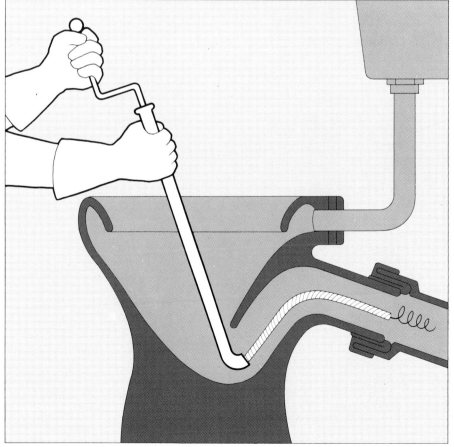

Unclogging the Main Drains

When the water draining from one appliance wells up through the waste of another, the trouble probably lies in the main drain or its branches, which channel waste into the sewer. Since waste flows downwards, any blockage in the main drain or soil stack will stop up all the appliances above that point. In addition, anything that blocks the vent, which keeps air flowing through the system, will cause waste to drain away sluggishly, and there may be an unpleasant odour in the house.

Before starting work, plot the course of the pipes in your waste system to help you pinpoint the blockage. You may find it helpful to sketch the layout on paper. Once you have decided where the obstruction might be, try a rubber plunger *(page 18)* on the appliance closest to the trouble spot—this can be effective even if the blockage is in the main soil and waste stack.

If that fails, try cleaning out the stack with a cleaning rod or drain auger. Work from the appliance closest to the blockage, following the instructions on page 20. To make the job easier, hire an electric auger up to 30 metres long from a tool-hire firm.

Even an electric auger, however, will not work effectively if it has to go round too many bends. Always take the straightest possible route to the problem area. In the main stack that usually means working through the nearest inspection chamber or, more commonly, through a cleaning eye *(opposite page, above)*. A blockage below ground level, in the drain to the sewer, will have to be reached through a gully or inspection chamber *(opposite page, below)*.

In most plumbing repairs speed is essential, but unclogging the main drains calls instead for patience. Avoid precipitate action. The column of water trapped by the blockage may extend above the point where your cleaning eye is located, and it will gush out as soon as you open the eye. Wait for at least two or three hours after you have spotted the trouble before starting work, to allow as much as possible of the waste to seep past the blockage. Even then, you will need mops, buckets, rags and old newspapers to soak up any overflow. When you have finished clearing up, dispose of the rags and newspapers in sealed plastic bags and disinfect the site.

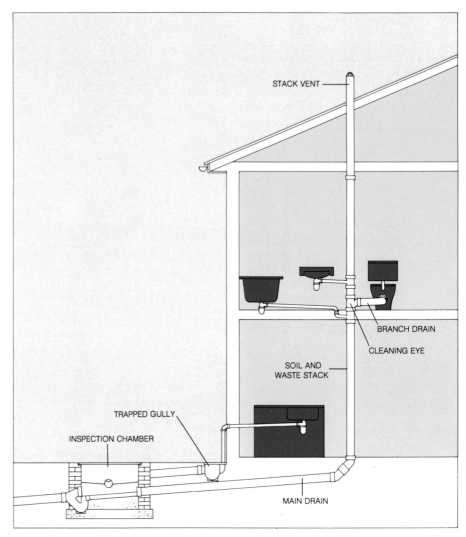

STACK VENT

BRANCH DRAIN

CLEANING EYE

SOIL AND WASTE STACK

TRAPPED GULLY

INSPECTION CHAMBER

MAIN DRAIN

Locating the blockage. The first step in finding blockages is to check which fittings are draining normally; clogs in a soil and waste stack will always be below the level of the lowest blocked fitting and above the highest working fitting. In the plumbing system above, a blockage near the cleaning eye would block both the basin and the W.C., but not the bath. Should all the first-floor fittings be blocked, the problem must lie below the point where the bath waste feeds into the stack. In either case, the blockage should be cleared through the cleaning eye *(opposite,*

above). If the sink on the ground floor is blocked, the fault must lie in the gully or the pipes leading to or from it. Try pouring water through the gully. If it passes freely through, the blockage is in the sink waste, which should be cleared through the sink trap; if not, clear the gully with a hose or auger *(opposite)*. When all the appliances are blocked, the blockage must be in the drain to the public sewer, and should be tackled through the inspection chamber. Often the first sign of such an obstruction will be flooding from the gully—the lowest drain outlet in the system.

Unblocking the Waste Stack

1 Opening the cleaning eye. Lay plenty of rags and newspapers on the floor around the waste stack before opening the cleaning eye, to help soak up any flooding. Undo the screws that hold the cleaning eye in place, then remove the plate.

2 Clearing the stack. Using a drain auger that is long enough to reach as far as your inspection chamber, probe for the obstruction and remove it by breaking through it or by drawing it out. When the water has drained away, flush the stack with a hose. Replace the plate on the cleaning eye and secure it with the screws.

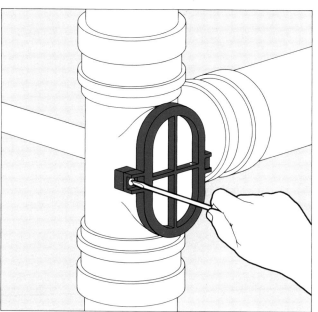

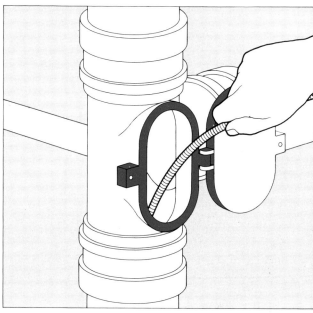

Clearing the Gully

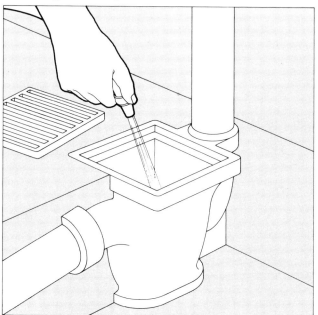

Using a hose. If an outside gully blocks and floods it is worth trying to flush it clear with a hose under mains pressure. The force of the water may disperse or eject the blockage, and the flooding if it fails to do so is less serious out of doors. If the treatment does not succeed, try clearing the obstruction with your hands, wearing rubber gloves. If this fails, use an auger.

Augering the Main Drain

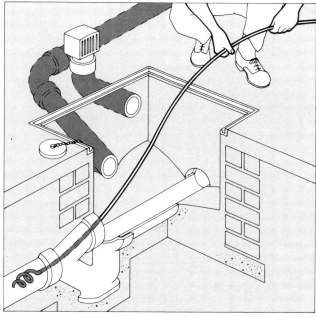

Working from the inspection chamber. Remove the cover and use an auger to clear the obstruction. If the chamber has a sewer-gas interceptor—a trap with a water seal to exclude drain smells— check the trap first to see if it is blocked. If not, remove the plug from the rodding arm to allow the auger to pass straight into the drain pipe without going through the bend of the trap.

2 Big Savings from Small Jobs

A costly drip. Stopping a drip from an old-fashioned bib tap *(left)* is one job that most home owners have learnt to do. Fixing more sophisticated modern taps is no more difficult—and prepares the owner for remedying a whole host of other plumbing problems, thus accomplishing a double saving: less wasted water and no cost at all for plumber's labour.

Almost any job seems difficult the first time you do it, whether it is making an omelette or putting a new flex on a lamp. The same is true of working on your house plumbing. A dripping tap is a rudimentary problem that can be baffling; you must work out how to get it apart—often the trickiest step of the operation—and what part is at fault. But once you have learnt to cope with the everyday problems that beset sinks, basins, W.C.s and baths, you will save money and the inconvenience of waiting for a plumber to come. Some jobs in the bathroom or kitchen a plumber may not do at all, such as replacing a broken tile or a cracked soap dish. Many other repairs are so simple that today's highly paid plumbers are reluctant to take them on; their time is more profitably spent on large projects.

Even those who think of themselves as all thumbs can master the steps involved in basic plumbing repairs. There are a few elementary guidelines that can make the task easier.

☐ Work slowly and be patient.

☐ Turn off the water supply. If you are working on a tap, put the plug in the waste to prevent screws and other small parts from falling down it.

☐ When you dismantle the parts of a fixture, line them up in the order and orientation of disassembly so you can put them back together more easily without wondering which way a part faces.

☐ Do not force a part "frozen" by corrosion; apply a few drops of penetrating oil, wait a while—overnight if necessary—and try again.

☐ Inspect parts for signs of wear or corrosion while you have a fitting dismantled. Replacing a worn part avoids future trouble and the necessity of dismantling the fixture or fitting again.

☐ Keep on hand a supply of common replacement parts—a selection of different-sized tap and float valve washers and O-rings. That way you avoid the bother of a special trip to buy them and the nuisance of leaving the water turned off while you are out matching the faulty part.

Finding the right replacement parts may be the most troublesome part of a plumbing repair. The best source is a plumbers' merchant, which will have a larger stock of fittings and more knowledgeable salespeople than a builders' merchant or hardware shop. Generally it is better to buy parts made by the manufacturer of your fixture; in some cases it is essential, for no others will fit.

Be prepared for frustration in the search for replacement parts. Although there is some standardization in fittings and fixtures, many manufacturers make several types of taps that differ slightly in design and sometimes in the way they operate. And since such equipment may last for decades, you may have a model for which parts are no longer available. If you cannot find a needed part, replace the whole fitting.

Tap Maintenance and Repair

The numerous taps in every modern home are expensive to replace, but with simple maintenance will last for many years. To do your own repairs promptly and economically, you need to know how the tap works and how to dismantle and reassemble it.

Taps can vary widely in appearance, but their external differences conceal basically similar structures. There are three main types of tap found in the home: bib taps, with a horizontal water inlet; pillar taps, with a vertical inlet; and mixer taps, comprising a hot and cold tap, designed as a single unit with a shared spout.

In the older designs of pillar tap there is a capstan-head handwheel and a bell-shaped "easy-clean" cover for the mechanism *(right)*; more recent types of pillar tap have a shrouded head, where a chrome-plated handwheel extends over and covers the interior down to the tap body *(opposite page, below)*.

The head or handwheel of the tap is connected to the top of a vertical spindle, of which the bottom 20 mm is threaded so that it can move up and down within the headgear nut. The outside of this nut is also threaded to screw into the body of the tap. Fixed into the end of the spindle is a small plastic rod and disc known as the jumper; the washer is attached to the end of the jumper, either by a small button or by a nut. The tap is closed by turning the handwheel to screw the spindle down, lowering the washer on to a raised metal flange—the seat—within the tap body. It is the contact of the washer and the seat that creates the tight seal that prevents water passing out through the spout. When the tap is turned on, the water is prevented from escaping up the tap body by a second nut—the gland nut—at the top of the spindle. The gland nut is packed with waterproof material, known as gland packing, to make an efficient seal.

Anatomy of a tap. The exploded diagram on the right reveals the secrets of a standard pillar tap with a capstan-head handwheel. In this illustration the gland nut is designed as an integral part of the easy-clean cover, and the washer is held in place by a small moulded button.

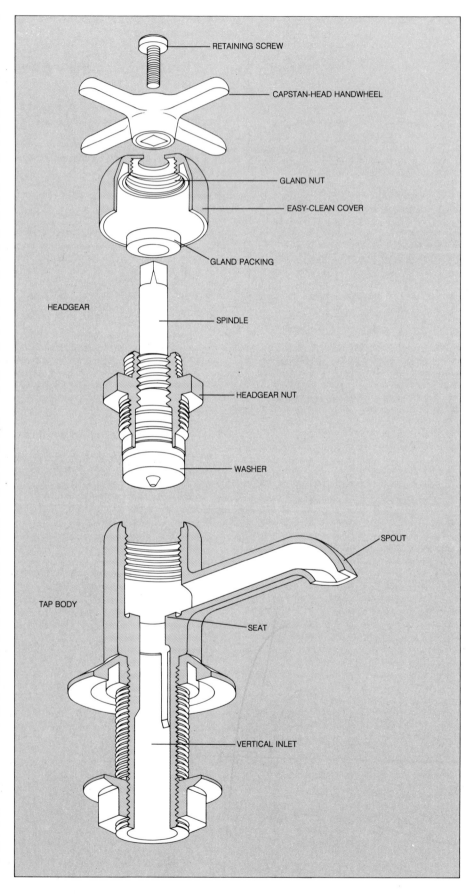

Removing a Capstan Head

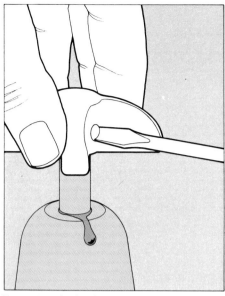

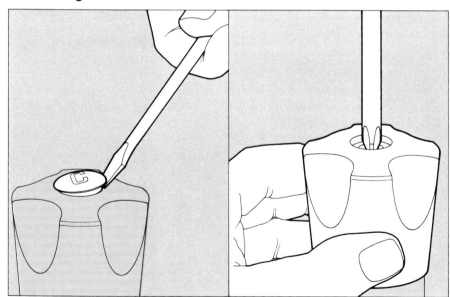

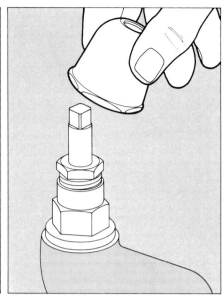

1 **Unscrewing the head.** The retaining screw that secures the tap head to the spindle may be located either at the side or on the top of the head itself. The screw may be either crosshead or single slot; select the appropriate screwdriver and undo the screw, putting it down in a safe place. Now lift off the head, exposing the top of the spindle.

2 **Tackling a stubborn head.** If the head is difficult to remove, open the tap completely, unscrew the easy-clean cover and raise it as far as possible. Slip two small blocks of wood between the base of the headgear nut and the cover, then turn the tap off. The upward pressure of the cover will push off the head.

3 **Exposing the headgear nut.** Lift off the easy-clean cover and set it on one side together with the tap head and retaining screw. The top of the spindle, the gland nut and the headgear nut are now exposed ready for the next stage.

Unscrewing a Shrouded Head

A Variant Form

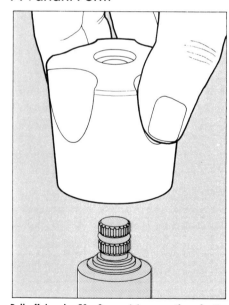

Locating the screw. The heads of shrouded-head taps may be held by a retaining screw concealed beneath the central plastic red or blue button on the head itself. Prise up the button with the tip of a screwdriver (*above*) and undo the exposed screw (*above, right*).

Pull-off heads. If after prising up the plastic button you discover there is no retaining screw underneath, you can remove the head by simply pulling it off (*above*). The exposed spindle of a shrouded-head tap looks slightly different from a capstan spindle: it is notched and circled by a tiny rubber ring—an O-ring—in order to give a secure purchase to the head.

Dealing with a Dripping Tap

A dripping tap is not only an irritation, it also stains and eventually erodes a sink or basin, and it can waste water surprisingly quickly. A steady drip usually results from one of three defects: a worn washer, defective gland packing or corrosion of the seat.

A worn washer is indicated by the continual dripping of the tap from the spout after it has been turned off. The temptation is to turn the tap off tighter and tighter each time, but inevitably, replacement of the washer becomes necessary, and it is better done sooner rather than later.

Failure of the gland packing is a common and often neglected fault. Water leaks up the spindle when the tap is turned on, and trickles down over the easy-clean cover or, in the case of shrouded-head taps, over the tap body itself. In hard water areas especially the bright chrome plating soon becomes dulled with lime deposits, which can be very difficult to remove. The gland packing can be renewed either with graphite-impregnated twine, which is manufactured in different sizes especially for this purpose, or with PTFE tape *(opposite)*.

If the tap still continues to drip after you have renewed the washer, then the tap seat is probably at fault. Over a period of time it can become pitted by corrosion so that it fails to make a good seal with the washer. This problem can be overcome by grinding the surface of the seat smooth with a special tool available at a plumbers' merchant or a tool-hire firm. The tool is screwed down into the tap body so that its cutting edge contacts the upper surface of the seat. The corroded surface can then be planed or cut smooth again by turning the tool *(opposite page)*.

Before starting any tap repair, turn off the water supply at the point closest to the fixture you are working on. Then turn on the tap to allow any remaining water to run out of the pipe. So that you do not scar the chrome, use a smooth-jawed spanner rather than a toothed one, or protect the chrome with a piece of cloth.

Put the plug into the basin or sink so that small parts do not get lost, and line a basin with a towel to prevent any damage from dropped parts or tools. Place the parts aside in the exact order they were removed so that they will be easy to reassemble.

Replacing the Washer

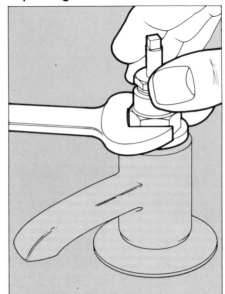

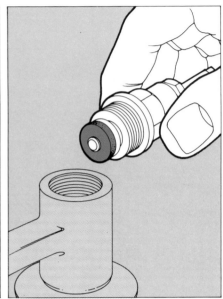

1 **Unscrewing the headgear nut.** Using an open-ended spanner of the correct size or a smooth-jawed adjustable spanner, unscrew the headgear nut, which is visible immediately above the tap body after you have removed the easy-clean cover or shrouded head *(previous page)*.

2 **Exposing the washer.** Once the headgear nut has been loosened, lift out the entire assembly. The complete headgear will now be visible together with the defective washer.

Undoing a Washer Nut

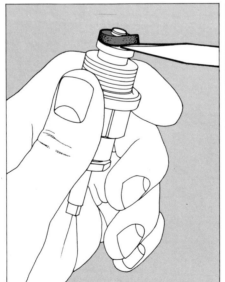

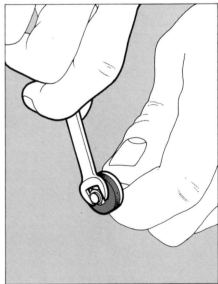

3 **Removing the washer.** In most cases the washer is attached to the jumper by means of a small button. The washer can be prised off the jumper with the tip of a screwdriver. Replace the old washer with a new one of the correct size.

Removing the nut. If the washer is secured to the jumper by a tiny nut, use a spanner of exactly the right size to undo the nut and replace the washer in the normal way. If the nut is difficult to undo, apply penetrating oil, wait a while and try again. In some cases, the jumper and washer are not fixed into the spindle but may remain on the seating when the tap body is removed.

Using a Tap-Reseating Tool

Smoothing a tap seat. Should the seating be pitted or scratched so that it fails to make a tight seal with the washer, grind the tap seat smooth with a special reseating tool. Once the cutting edge is in contact with the seat it will need only one or two turns to smooth it. Take care not to plane away too much of the seat.

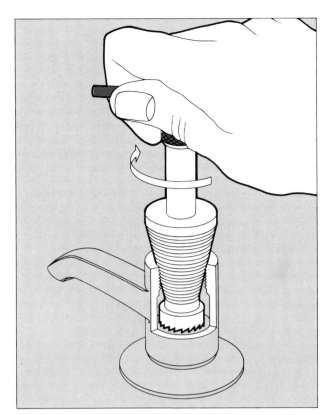

Renewing the Gland Packing

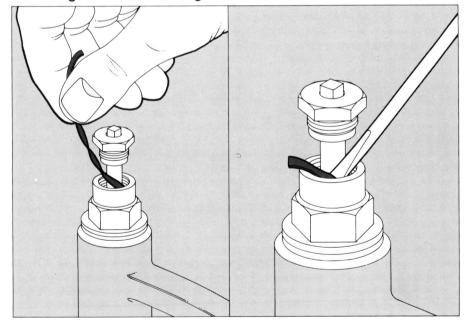

Taping the gland nut. If the gland packing which sits between the gland nut and the spindle has become worn or compressed so that the seal is faulty, renew it with plastic PTFE tape. After removing the tap head to expose the gland nut, twist a length of PTFE tape into a cord, loosen and lift the gland nut on the spindle *(above, left)*, and push the PTFE tape down into the cavity with the tip of a screwdriver *(above, right)*. Then screw the gland nut down again and replace the tap head.

Replacing an O-Ring

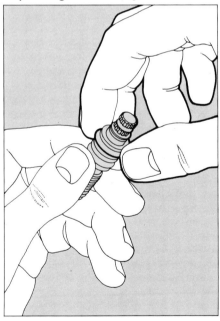

Resealing the spindle. Some mixer taps do not have conventional gland packing but use small rubber rings instead—O-rings—as a seal on the spindle. These can be pulled off the spindle by hand and replaced with new ones very easily. Make sure the replacements are the same size.

A Reverse-Pressure Tap

The simplest of all taps to re-washer and repair is a reverse-pressure tap commonly known by its trade name, "Supatap". This tap can be re-washered without any need to turn off the mains water supply. Disassembly and reassembly of the tap are unusually straightforward and the interior of the tap is easily accessible.

The curved water inlet arm of the reverse-pressure tap is connected to a relatively short tap body. To turn the tap on or off you turn the tap body itself, using the lugs attached, with the same action as for a conventional tap.

For re-washering, the tap body is unscrewed completely in two simple steps *(Steps 1 and 2, opposite page)*. Since the unscrewing action is similar to turning the tap on, the water flow increases temporarily, then stops abruptly as a check valve falls into position and is held in place by the pressure of the water behind it.

Before re-washering the tap, you should line the basin with a towel to prevent damage from accidentally dropped parts. To facilitate reassembly, lay the parts on the floor beside the basin in the order in which you removed them.

It is important to buy identical replacement parts made only by the manufacturer of the reverse-pressure tap. Sizes will vary depending on whether the tap is a sink, basin or bath model. If your local plumbers' merchant cannot supply the part, contact the manufacturer.

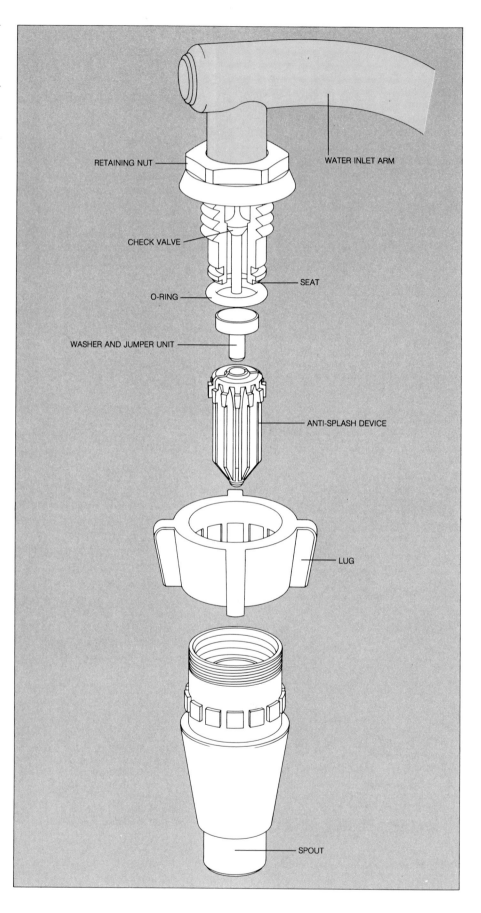

Inside the reverse-pressure tap. The tap body conceals a check valve, a washer and jumper unit and an anti-splash device. When the tap is turned on, the washer is lowered so that water can pass from the water inlet arm through the tap body and out through the spout. When the tap is turned off, the washer is forced against a tap seat at the base of the water inlet arm, thus cutting off the flow of water.

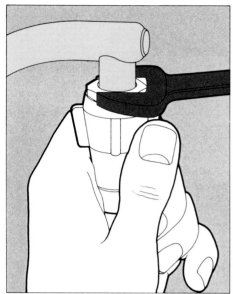

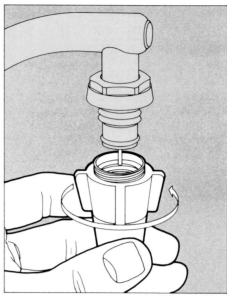

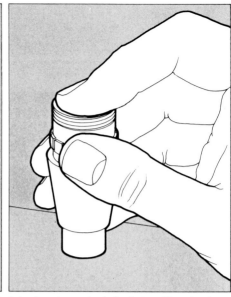

1 **Removing the retaining nut.** With the tap turned off, locate the retaining nut that connects the water inlet arm to the tap body. Using a spanner, turn the nut in an anti-clockwise direction *(above)*, until the nut reaches the top of its thread.

2 **Dismantling the tap body.** Grasp the water inlet arm so that the loosened retaining nut is held free of the tap body. With your other hand, rotate the tap lugs as if you were turning the tap on. Keep turning until the tap body comes away in your hand *(above)*.

3 **Releasing the anti-splash device.** Slip the lug fitting off the tap body. Tap the spout firmly on a hard, shatterproof surface (not the basin). Turn the tap body upside-down; the brass anti-splash device, which is attached to the washer and jumper fitting, will fall out.

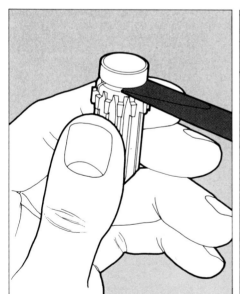

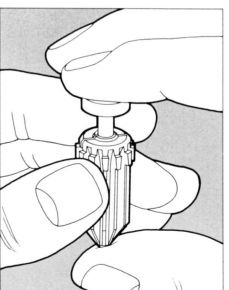

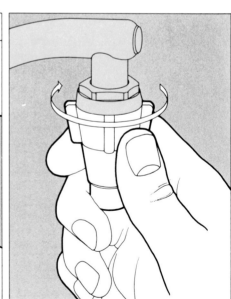

4 **Removing the washer and jumper.** The rubber washer is contained within the brass cap of the jumper fitting at the top of the anti-splash device. Insert a penknife blade or screwdriver underneath the cap *(above)* and carefully prise out the worn fitting. Discard the washer and jumper fitting.

5 **Fitting the new washer.** With your fingers, press the new washer and jumper fitting securely into the anti-splash device *(above)*. The tap is now ready for reassembly.

6 **Reassembling the tap.** With the rubber washer uppermost, drop the anti-splash device back into the tap body. Slip the lug fitting on to the tap. Gripping the lugs, screw the tap body clockwise back into position *(above)*. Use a spanner to tighten the retaining nut against the tap body.

Simple and Versatile: the Bath/ Shower Mixer

In place of the basic pillar taps on the bath, many homes have a bath/shower mixer, an economical and convenient fitting that provides the option of a shower without the expense of a separate installation. The mixer makes it possible to blend the hot and cold supplies to the right temperature in a single spout, and to direct the flow either straight into the bath or through a hose and spray head for a shower.

A mixer must be fitted according to the regulations that require that the water pressure in hot and cold supplies must be equal—in practice, that they should both be indirect *(page 13)*, and that the hot water cylinder should be supplied from the same cold water cistern that supplies the cold water separately to the mixer. It is illegal to take the cold water supply direct from the mains, since unexpected fluctuations in the mains pressure would upset the balance in the mixer and might scald someone using the shower; there would also be a risk of back-siphonage.

Maintenance of the bath/shower mixer is simple once you understand its principle of operation *(right)*. The internal design of all models is similar in spite of the variety of styles. The most usual faults that develop are due to wear in the O-rings that provide the seals in the combined valve. Water may leak from the underside of the diverter button, or continue to drip—or even flow—from the tap spout when the button is in the "shower" position. Conversely, water may drip from the shower when the button is in the "tap" position. These faults can be remedied by replacing the worn O-rings—a straightforward repair demonstrated on the opposite page. If water drips from the spout when the taps are closed, then one (or both) of the taps will need re-washering *(pages 26–28)*.

The mechanism of a bath/shower diverter. The mechanism consists of a spring and a spindle with a rubber disc or washer that fits into the diverter body. Normally, the spring holds the washer in position to seal the outlet to the hose. When the diverter button is pulled up, the resistance of the spring is overcome and the washer seals the outlet to the tap. Water pressure holds the washer in place until the flow is turned off.

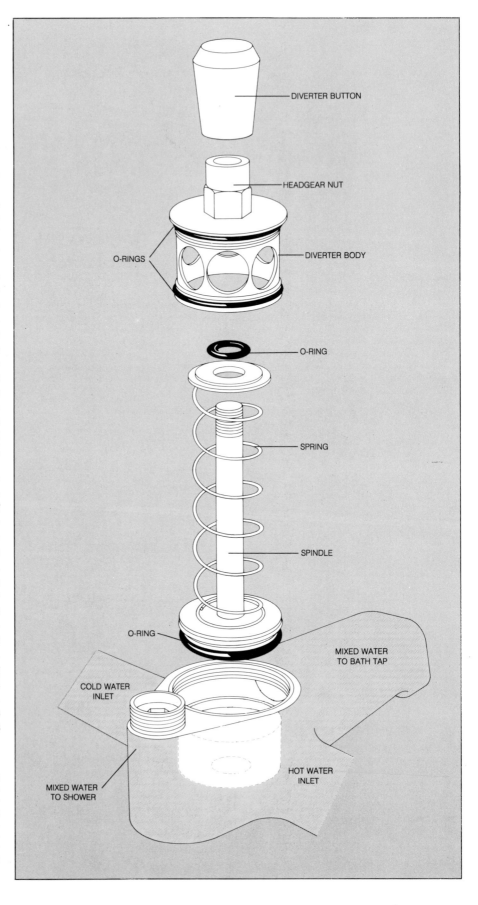

DIVERTER BUTTON

HEADGEAR NUT

O-RINGS

DIVERTER BODY

O-RING

SPRING

SPINDLE

O-RING

MIXED WATER TO BATH TAP

COLD WATER INLET

HOT WATER INLET

MIXED WATER TO SHOWER

1 **Loosening the mechanism.** Raise the diverter button on top of the unit with one hand. With a spanner, loosen the headgear nut that holds the diverter button in position *(right)* and lift out the entire diverter mechanism.

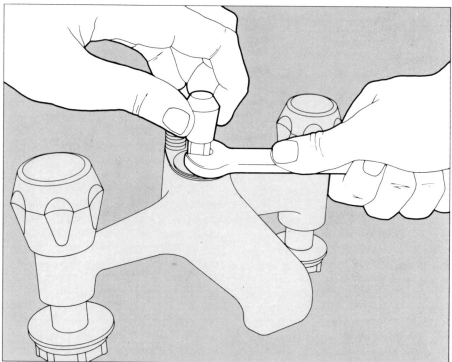

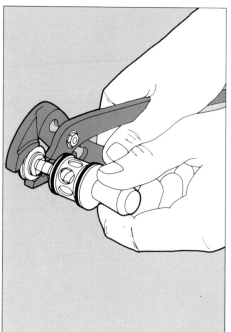

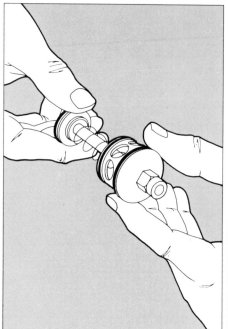

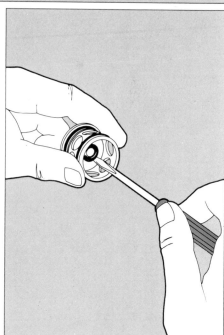

2 **Removing the button.** Using slip-joint pliers, grasp the disc at the base of the spindle and hold it steady. With your other hand, turn the diverter button anticlockwise to loosen it. Remove the button from the mechanism and set it aside in a safe place.

3 **Detaching the spindle.** Carefully withdraw the spindle from the spindle body, setting the spring safely to one side. You will see the mechanism shown opposite. All the O-rings will be easily accessible, except for the one housed between the top of the spindle and the underside of the diverter body. It is worth replacing all the O-rings at the same time: if one is worn, the others are likely to be also.

4 **Replacing the O-rings.** Remove all the O-rings; use the tip of a screwdriver to pick out the small O-ring under the diverter body *(above)*. Fit new O-rings of the correct size into position, pushing them into place with the screwdriver tip. Replace the diverter button. Reassemble the mechanism and place it back on top of the unit. Secure the nut to complete the repair.

Installing a Waste and Overflow Unit

Water delivered into sink, basin or bath has to escape again into the house drainage system, but the fittings required for outflow are less complex than those that bring the supply to each fixture. Since the drainage system operates by gravity alone, the fittings concerned—wastes, overflow pipes and traps—need not be able to stand up to mains water pressure, and they are easier to work with. In order to install them there is no need to switch off or drain down the water supply. Just make sure the taps are all securely turned off.

If you are installing a new fixture, you will of course need to know how to fit the waste and overflow systems for it. But even in an existing sink or basin it may be necessary to replace a damaged or corroded waste, with its combined overflow pipe. Many ceramic basins have an integrally designed overflow, but steel or plastic sinks and basins generally have a so-called "banjo-type" combined overflow and waste pipe. A flexible hose from the overflow inlet joins the waste at an elbow, making the banjo-shaped component that gives the fitting its name. The plug is attached by a chain to the end of the hose through the overflow inlet in the sink. Be sure that you buy a replacement waste that matches the diameter of your sink outlet hole.

To dismantle the existing waste, first unscrew with a spanner the large nut on the underside of the sink which connects the bottom of the waste to the trap, and remove the trap. If the trap is old and unsightly, you can decide to replace it as well *(page 38)*. With a wooden mallet, gently tap the underside of the waste to break the seal in the sink, and lift out the fitting. Unscrew the small threaded unit at the top of the overflow in the sink. Remove the complete overflow system, and you are ready to install your new fitting.

1 **Bedding the waste.** To seal the junction of the waste with the sink, make a 5 mm sandwich of two layers of putty enclosing a layer of plumber's jointing paste on the underside of the lip of the waste. Insert the waste in the sink outlet hole. Bed the waste down firmly and wipe away excess sealant. If your waste is supplied with a black rubber washer, use it instead of the putty and paste seal.

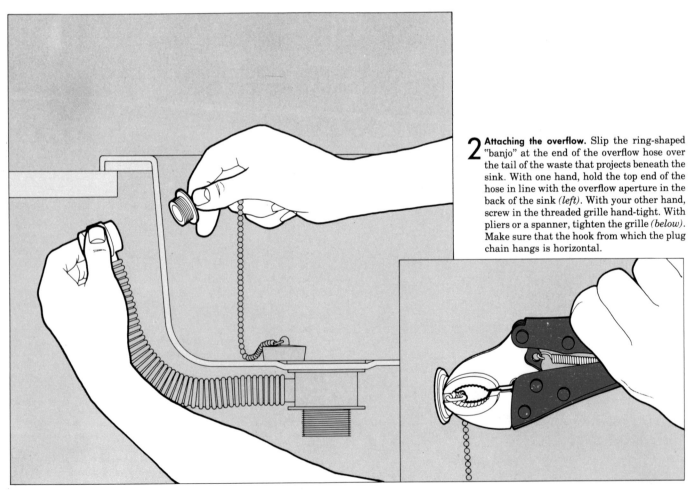

2 **Attaching the overflow.** Slip the ring-shaped "banjo" at the end of the overflow hose over the tail of the waste that projects beneath the sink. With one hand, hold the top end of the hose in line with the overflow aperture in the back of the sink *(left)*. With your other hand, screw in the threaded grille hand-tight. With pliers or a spanner, tighten the grille *(below)*. Make sure that the hook from which the plug chain hangs is horizontal.

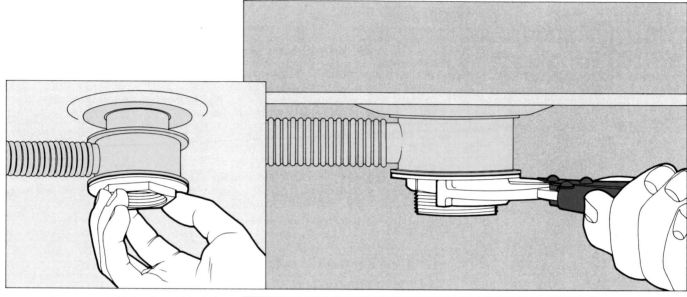

3 **Securing the waste.** To hold the elbow of the banjo in place, slip the washer and nut on to the tail of the waste and screw up the nut hand-tight. When you have checked that the parts are all positioned correctly, tighten the nut with a spanner. To hold it steady as you tighten it, get a helper to press down on the waste in the sink—or do it yourself if you have long enough arms. Do not overtighten the nut or you may distort the banjo and impair the watertight seal.

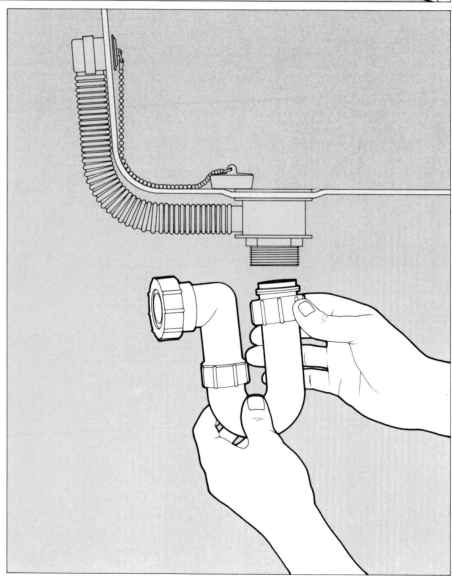

4 **Replacing the trap.** If you are using the original trap, wash it out and fix it back in place. If you are installing a new trap *(page 38)*, attach it first to the tail of the waste with its own compression nut, then make the connection to the waste pipe, in this case also with a compression joint. Then fill the sink with water to test the joint between waste and sink. Let the water run into the overflow for several minutes, then remove the plug to allow the water to flow out through the waste. During this operation check all joints for leaks, then tighten or remake any defective joints.

Adjusting and Replacing a Basin Pop-up

The seal of a pop-up waste—a metal plug closing upon a metal flange, or ring—is never quite as watertight as that of an old-style rubber plug. Moreover, the pop-up mechanism has several moving parts and needs periodic adjustments. But the pop-up's convenience has made it quite popular and a householder should learn to cope with its malfunctions. They are, fortunately, few in number: a plug that fails to open or close properly, and the enemies of all drainage systems—blockages and leaks.

Pop-up problems are usually caused by faulty connections. The control knob on top of the basin is part of a three-section linkage: a vertical lift rod; another vertical rod, flat and pierced by holes, called a clevis; and a seesaw-like horizontal rod that pivots on a plastic ball inside the waste to raise and lower the plug. Adjusting the mechanism calls for two simple settings on the lift rod and clevis.

Loose hair and similar debris are the usual causes of clogging. To clear the waste you must remove the plug, either by lifting or twisting it out of the basin or by dismantling the pivot rod (*opposite page, above*). When you have freed the plug, clean it, then clear out the waste below with a brush or piece of cloth wrapped round stiff wire, such as coat hanger wire.

There are two kinds of leaks. Water that drips or trickles from the mechanism beneath the basin is leaking around the pivot ball. Tighten the retaining nut that holds the ball in place; if that does not work, remove the nut and then replace the pivot-ball washer. Water that seeps down the outside of the waste is a more serious matter. The thudding of the plug against the flange may have broken the putty seal beneath the flange; by loosening a lock nut under the bowl you can raise the flange and renew the seal. More often, this type of leak is due to corrosion of one of the parts of the waste—a sure signal that the waste will soon fail completely. To fix the leak properly, you should replace the entire waste assembly (*opposite page, below*).

1 Setting the lift rod. If the pop-up plug does not make a good seal in the closed position, begin your adjustment with the lift rod—the vertical shaft that runs down from the control knob and through the top of the basin. Pull the knob as far up as you can, and free the rod by loosening the clevis screw with a pair of tape-wrapped pliers (*below*). Press the pop-up plug down to seal the waste (the clevis rod will rise slightly) and retighten the clevis screw. You may find that the pop-up mechanism is now slightly jammed and difficult to operate; if so, go on to Step 2.

2 Setting the pivot rod. With your fingers, squeeze the spring clip that holds the pivot rod in the clevis to free the pivot rod completely. Reset the rod one hole higher up, threading it through the spring clip on both sides of the clevis. Try the pop-up mechanism; if necessary, repeat Step 1.

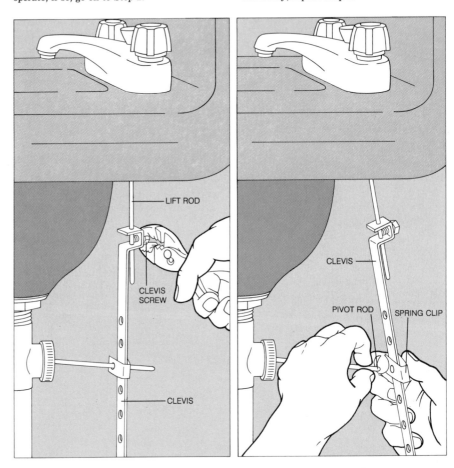

A medley of pop-up plugs. These four common types of pop-up plugs all do the same job, but the methods of installing and removing them differ widely. Numbers 1 and 2 rest on the inside end of the pivot rod; to remove either of them, raise the plug to the open position and lift it out of the waste. Number 3 engages the rod in a slot, and comes free of the rod with a quarter turn anticlockwise. If you cannot remove your pop-up plug by lifting or turning, it must resemble Number 4, which engages the rod in a loop like the eye of a huge needle. To disengage this plug, you must free the pivot rod from the clevis and pull it partly or completely out of the waste T underneath the basin (*opposite page, above*).

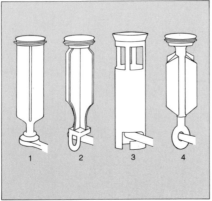

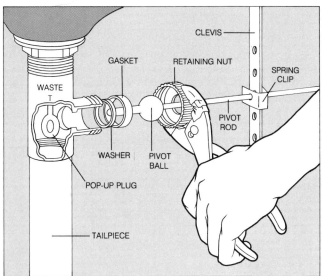

The pivot-rod assembly. With a tape-wrapped adjustable spanner or pliers, unscrew the retaining nut that secures the pivot-rod assembly inside the waste T. Squeeze the spring clip on the clevis and draw the pivot rod out of the T. You can now pull the plug out for cleaning.

To stop leaks or to install a new assembly, follow the same procedure as in the first step in dismantling a pop-up *(opposite page, top)*. A leak at the retaining nut may be stopped by tightening the nut, but check the gasket and washer inside the pivot ball for wear and, if necessary, replace them. The remainder of the dismantling and installation procedure is described below.

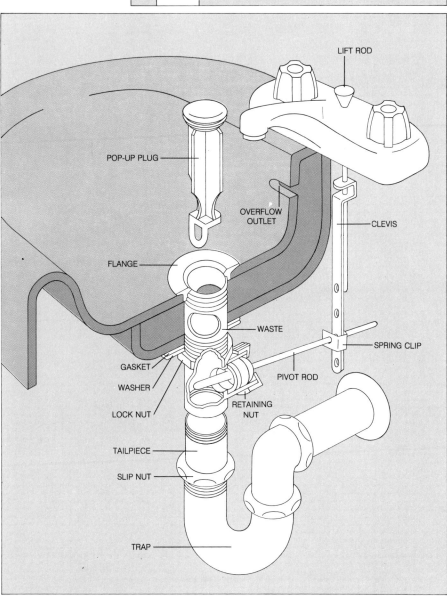

Replacing the waste. Start a replacement job by freeing the pivot rod from the waste T *(above)*. Unscrew the slip nut that fastens the tailpiece to the trap, then unscrew the tailpiece from the waste and push it down into the trap, out of the way. Loosen the lock nut that secures the waste underneath the basin, and unscrew the waste from the flange. An old, corroded waste will be hard to budge at first; do not hesitate to apply pressure with the spanner, even if you flatten the waste a bit. Inside the basin, prise up the flange with the blade of a knife or the tip of a screwdriver; be careful not to scar the basin's surface. Scrape away the putty at the mouth of the waste and wipe it clean with a dry cloth. Discard the old tailpiece (a new one will come with the new waste assembly) but keep the slip nut that fastened it to the trap; replace the slip nut washer if it is badly worn.

Use tape-wrapped spanners for all steps of the installation job. Start by setting a slip nut and a washer on the new tailpiece and pushing the piece down into the trap. Apply a thin layer of plumber's putty under the rim of the flange, and press the flange into place in the mouth of the waste. Coat the threads of the waste and tailpiece with jointing compound, screw the waste into the flange and the tailpiece into the waste, and tighten the tailpiece slip nut on to the trap. Finally, tighten the lock nut against the washer and gasket with an adjustable spanner. Caution: do not overtighten this nut or the porcelain above it may crack.

If you are replacing the pop-up mechanism as well as the waste, feed the pivot rod into the waste T and tighten the retaining nut. Insert the lift rod down through the tap body or the top of the basin and fasten its lower end to the clevis with the clevis screw. Feed the pivot rod through a clevis hole, making it fast with the spring clip. Try the mechanism and, if necessary, reset the lift rod and clevis *(opposite page, top)*.

Replacing Sink and Basin Traps

Below every single plumbing fixture that drains into the house system is a trap containing a water seal, intended to prevent the return of foul gases from the sewer into the living areas of house or garden. The trap takes the form of a small U-shaped loop of pipe so formed that it is always filled with water. As new water drains from the fixture it displaces the water in the trap; part of the outgoing water then remains in the loop to replace the seal and maintain the barrier against air that would otherwise drift back up from the drainage pipes.

The primary purpose of a trap is to prevent contamination from the drains, but it also provides a convenient means of access to the pipes below the fixture. If you have to unblock a pipe *(page 18)* you have an alternative to working through the plughole of the fixture.

A trap is also a safety measure against the loss of small valuable objects that get accidentally washed down the plughole: a ring or a contact lens can often be found lying safely at the bottom of the U-bend, and can simply be tipped out once you have removed the trap.

Traps in which the horizontal pipe leading from the U-bend gives a resemblance to the letter P are called P-traps. You will also often find S-traps, with a vertical pipe after the bend, and self-contained bottle-traps *(opposite page, below)* whose neat appearance makes them particularly popular for use under wash basins or anywhere else where they are openly visible.

Traps may be made in any of the normal plumbing materials, such as copper, steel, chrome or plastic. It is usually desirable that the material of the trap and the following waste pipe should match, but a new plastic trap can be satisfactorily fixed to an existing pipe of any material, as in the demonstrations on these pages. The same technique is used for attaching traps of both matching and dissimilar materials.

Fitting a Replacement P-Trap

Removing the old metal trap. To remove a copper or lead trap, first saw through the pipe with a hacksaw just behind the connecting nut *(below)*, so that you remove the threaded end of the pipe with the trap, creating a plain pipe end for fitting to the replacement trap. Next, with a spanner, unscrew the waste outlet nut that connects the top of the trap to the waste.

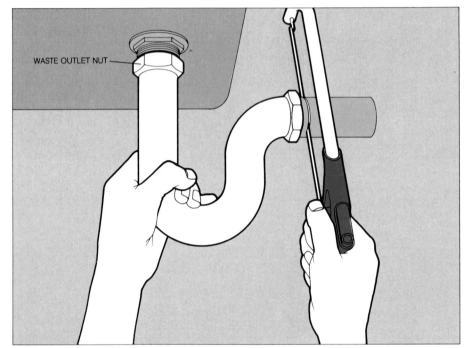

WASTE OUTLET NUT

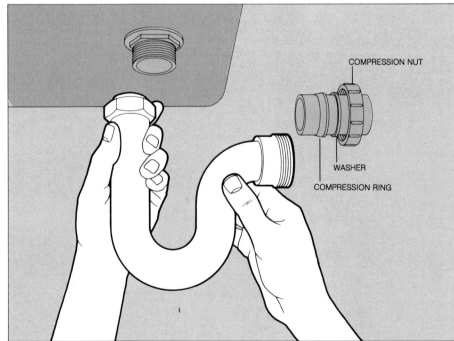

COMPRESSION NUT

WASHER

COMPRESSION RING

Fitting the plastic trap. Position the trap under the waste and screw its plastic nut on to the threaded tail. Hand-tighten the nut. To connect the bottom of the trap to the waste pipe, slip the components of the compression fitting supplied with the trap on to the sawn-off end of pipe: a threaded nut, a plastic washer and a rubber ring, in that order. Insert the end of the pipe in the outlet of the trap and screw the plastic nut home hand-tight on to the threaded end of the trap. Tighten the nuts at top and bottom of the trap with a pipe wrench, but do not overtighten them.

An Adaptable Two-Part Trap

The Simplest Connection

Fitting a swivel P-trap. To give greater flexibility in situations where the sink waste and the waste pipe are not well aligned, you may want to use a swivel P-trap to solve the problem. This trap is constructed in two parts: the small elbow *(inset)*, which is fitted to the waste pipe by means of its compression joint, and the U-bend section itself. The U-bend section is attached first to the threaded tail of the sink waste and then to the free end of the short elbow.

Making a push-fit joint. Plastic traps are also available with a push-fit connection to the drainage pipe. The trap connects to the sink or basin waste in the usual way with a compression nut, but to make the connection to the waste pipe, simply push home the pipe end into the outlet of the trap, where it is gripped by an integral rubber ring that lies within a groove.

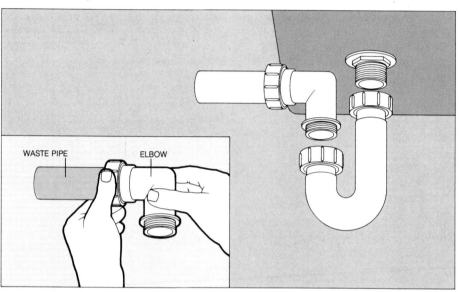

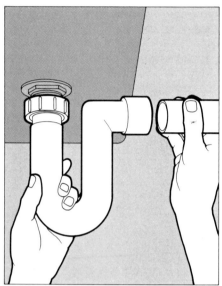

Fitting a Bottle-Trap

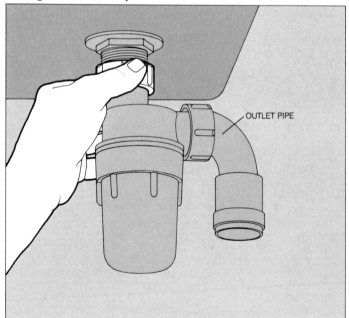

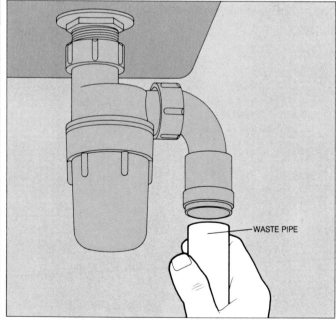

1 **Positioning the trap.** Attach the bottle-trap to the threaded tail of the sink waste by screwing up the plastic compression nut by hand. The outlet pipe, connected to the trap by a similar compression joint, need not be detached for fitting.

2 **Attaching the trap to the waste pipe.** Attach the waste pipe to the trap by pushing it into the end of the outlet pipe, until it is gripped firmly by the integral rubber ring seal. Most bottle-traps have a simple push-fit joint at the outlet. Tighten the compression nuts carefully with a spanner.

Keeping Your W.C. Cistern in Working Order

One of the most common minor plumbing problems is a W.C. cistern that will not function properly. Sometimes a cistern fails to empty efficiently, at other times it will not refill properly: either the water flows in too slowly, or the cistern overfills, causing a constant trickle from the overflow pipe. It is usually possible to fix both these annoying problems yourself.

Most modern W.C.s have a low-level cistern mounted behind the pan, either fitted directly on to the W.C. pan (close-coupled) or joined to the pan by a short flush pipe. When the flushing arm is operated or the chain is pulled, a siphonic action is initiated that empties the water from the cistern down the flush pipe and through the pan. The component parts of the flushing mechanism are shown below.

The usual cause of a failure to flush properly is a worn diaphragm, which does not seal the mouth of the siphon efficiently when the metal plate is raised by the flushing arm. Water escapes round the edges of the diaphragm instead of being carried upwards to start the siphonic action, and the flushing arm may have to be jerked two or three times before it will work. If the flushing mechanism completely fails, the wire linking the arm to the top of the siphon may be detached or broken.

Replacing a diaphragm and a link wire are simple repairs *(opposite)*. If a leak has developed in the siphon crown, however, it may be necessary to replace the entire siphon. Problems with refilling the cistern are usually due to a faulty float valve; three different types of float valve are described on the following pages.

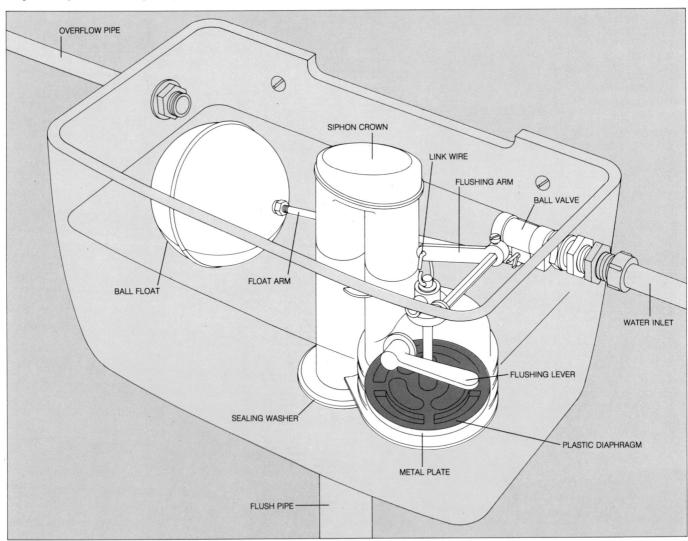

OVERFLOW PIPE

SIPHON CROWN

LINK WIRE

FLUSHING ARM

BALL VALVE

FLOAT ARM

BALL FLOAT

WATER INLET

FLUSHING LEVER

SEALING WASHER

PLASTIC DIAPHRAGM

METAL PLATE

FLUSH PIPE

The siphonic action of a W.C. cistern. When the flushing arm raises the metal plate or disc inside the wider end of the inverted U-shaped siphon, the plastic diaphragm resting on top of the plate is pressed down by the weight of the water above. This action effectively seals the inlet holes in the plate and carries the water upwards into the siphon crown to initiate the siphonic action that empties water from the cistern. When the cistern has been emptied and the water level has fallen low enough to let air enter the siphon crown and break the siphonic action, the metal plate sinks down again. As the cistern refills, water can flow up through the holes in the plate past the diaphragm, restoring the original situation.

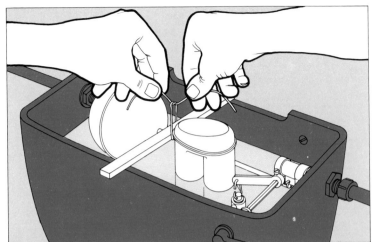

Replacing a Worn Diaphragm

1 Tying up the float arm. To immobilize the float arm, lay a strip of wood across the top of the cistern and tie the float arm to the wood with a piece of string *(left)*. If the arm were to drop with the water level, the ball valve would open again and allow in more water. When you have secured the float arm, flush the cistern.

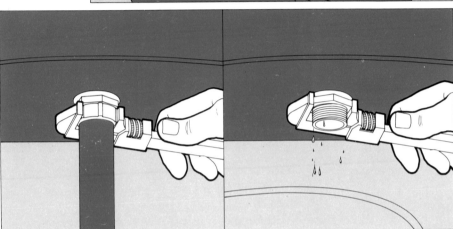

2 Emptying the cistern. Place a bowl beneath the cistern. Using an adjustable spanner, unscrew the large hexagonal nut that holds the flush pipe in position *(far left)*. Carefully detach the flush pipe from the cistern. The nut that secures the siphon will now be accessible. As you unscrew the siphon-retaining nut, the small amount of water remaining in the cistern will empty into the bowl *(left)*.

Replacing a Link Wire

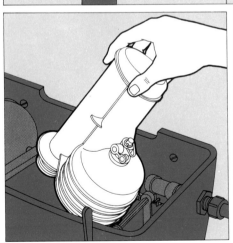

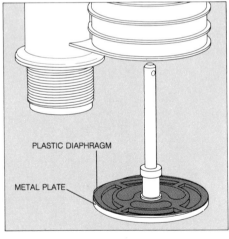

PLASTIC DIAPHRAGM

METAL PLATE

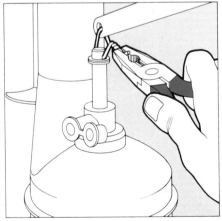

Making a new wire. Remove and discard the defective link wire. If it has fallen off, retrieve it from the bottom of the cistern; do not leave it there to corrode. With pliers, cut a new piece of stout wire 10 cm long—taken if you like from a wire coat hanger. Insert the wire through the hole in the lever arm, then thread it through the hole in the top of the lift rod. Use pliers to twist the ends of the wire together *(above)*.

3 Removing the siphon. Detach the flushing arm and lift out the siphon from the cistern *(above)*. If the siphon does not lift away easily, you may find that the siphon is secured by bolts inside the base of the cistern. Locate the bolts and remove them. (If your cistern is close-coupled you should be able to remove the metal plate without having to remove the siphon.)

4 Replacing the diaphragm. From the base of the larger tube that forms the siphon's U shape, remove the circular metal plate or disc, complete with its vertical rod *(above)*. Remove the thin plastic diaphragm and discard it. Fit a new diaphragm over the rod and slip it down to rest on the plate, covering it completely. Reassemble the mechanism and connect the flush pipe.

Float Valves

The level of the water in a W.C. cistern is controlled by a float valve, which is operated by a rigid metal or plastic arm terminating in a float (usually spherical). When the water level in the cistern drops as the W.C. is flushed, the float falls with the water, altering the angle of the rigid arm so that it opens the valve and allows in water. As the water level rises again the float is carried up with it until the arm is restored to its uppermost position, closing the valve and shutting off the water.

The differences between a washered ball valve (*right*), a diaphragm float valve (*opposite*) and a diaphragm/equilibrium valve (*overleaf*) are illustrated in exploded diagrams. When a cistern overfills it is usually because the washer or diaphragm is worn and fails to seal the valve when the float arm rises. Replacing the worn seal is normally enough to correct the fault. Two further expedients are illustrated overleaf: adjusting the water level in the cistern and making running repairs on a ball valve float that has lost its buoyancy.

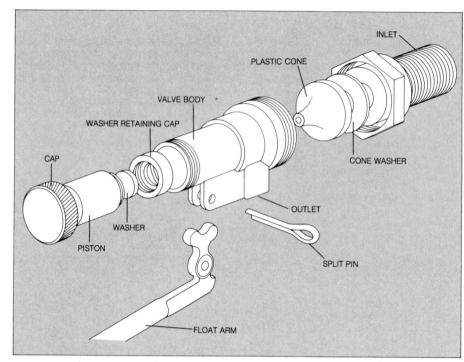

A washered ball valve. When the float arm rises, a washered piston, which moves horizontally within the valve body, is pressed against a valve seating—usually a removable plastic cone—to close off the incoming supply of water·once the cistern is full. The valve body pivots on a split pin; during the flushing operation, the downward movement of the float arm forces the piston and washer away from the cone, allowing water to flow through the outlet to refill the cistern.

Replacing the Washer of a Ball Valve

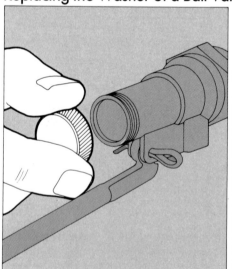

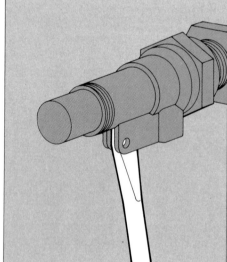

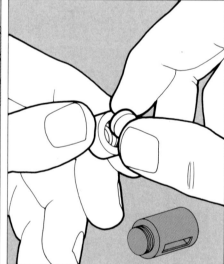

1 **Unscrewing the cap.** Turn off the water supply and remove the lid of the cistern. Unscrew the metal cap at the end of the valve body (*above*) and set it aside. To release the float arm, use pliers to straighten and withdraw the split pin. Set aside the pin and the arm.

2 **Removing the plug.** Beneath the valve body, locate the slot from which the float arm was removed; this slot lines up with a corresponding slot in the washered piston housed within the body. Insert the tip of a screwdriver and work the piston out of the end of the valve body (*above*). Be ready to catch the piston.

3 **Re-washering a two-part piston.** With pliers, unscrew the washer-retaining cap from the piston. Use your fingers to remove the worn washer (*above*). Install a new washer of carefully matched size. Reassemble all the parts.

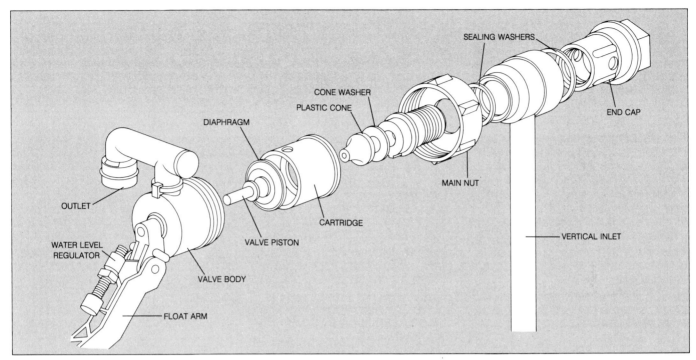

SEALING WASHERS

CONE WASHER

PLASTIC CONE

DIAPHRAGM

END CAP

OUTLET

MAIN NUT

WATER LEVEL
REGULATOR

VALVE PISTON

CARTRIDGE

VERTICAL INLET

VALVE BODY

FLOAT ARM

A diaphragm float valve. The distinctive feature of the diaphragm float valve is a large rubber disc that performs the same function as the washer in the more traditional ball valve shown on the opposite page. The outside of the rubber disc, or diaphragm, flexes against the walls of a cartridge enclosed in the valve body; when the float arm rises, the reinforced centrepiece of the diaphragm is pressed against the water inlet cone, shutting off the incoming water supply. The model shown above has a vertical inlet, but might equally well be attached to a horizontal inlet of the type shown opposite. The overhead water outlet is designed to reduce the noise of refilling the cistern.

Replacing the Diaphragm

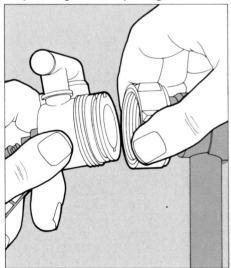
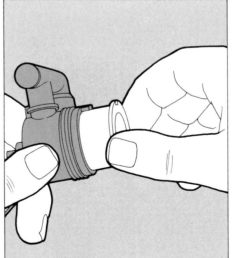
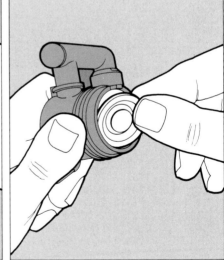

1 Unscrewing the retaining nut. When you have turned off the water supply and removed the lid of the cistern, locate the main nut of the float valve. Unscrew the nut to free it from the valve body *(above)* and gain access to the cartridge contained within.

2 Removing the cartridge. Withdraw the cartridge, which is held in position by a tongue-and-groove joint *(above)*. The cartridge contains a plastic cone and cone washer. Take care not to allow the cone and washer to fall into the cistern. Set the cartridge aside.

3 Picking out the diaphgram. Insert the point of a penknife blade deep inside the valve body, and prise the black rubber diaphragm away from the valve piston. Once the diaphragm is dislodged, you can pick it out with your fingers *(above)*. Press the replacement diaphragm into the valve body. Reposition the cartridge and screw the valve body back in place with the retaining nut.

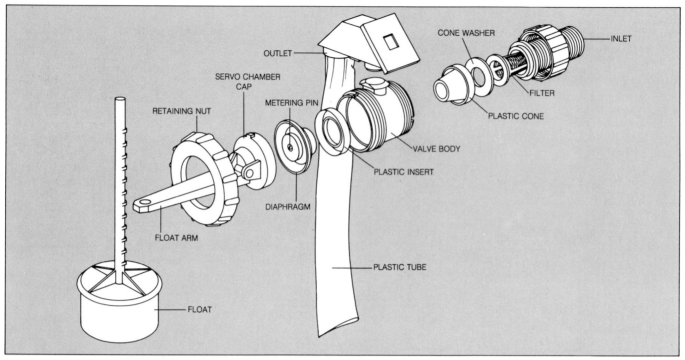

The diaphragm/equilibrium valve. This valve has a small servo chamber behind the diaphragm, through which a metering pin allows water to flow. Greater total pressure on the servo chamber side of the diaphragm closes the valve when the cistern is full. When the cistern is flushed, the float arm pivots downwards, opening a tiny hole—the pilot hole—that allows water to escape from the servo chamber, thus reducing the pressure on that side of the diaphragm. The incoming water then displaces the diaphragm and flows through the outlet. As the cistern refills the float arm pivots upwards, closing the pilot hole and re-establishing the pressure in the servo chamber. A plastic tube attached to the outlet allows the cistern to refill silently; the water level can be adjusted by changing the height at which the float arm is attached to the float.

Replacing the Diaphragm

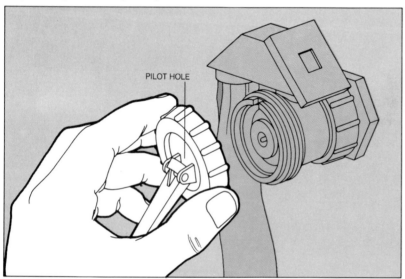

1 Unscrewing the float arm. Turn off the water supply and remove the lid of the cistern. Unscrew the retaining nut that holds the servo chamber cap in place. As the nut becomes free, so too will the cap, which is attached to the float arm (above). Clean the pilot hole in the centre of the servo chamber cap, and check that the washer or cushion on the float arm is not worn.

2 Removing the diaphragm. Insert the tip of a small screwdriver between the outer lip of the diaphragm and valve body, and pick out the worn diaphragm (above). Press the new diaphragm in place. Reposition the servo chamber cap and float arm, taking care that the tongue on the cap aligns with the groove on the valve body. Screw the retaining nut back into place.

Adjusting the Water Level

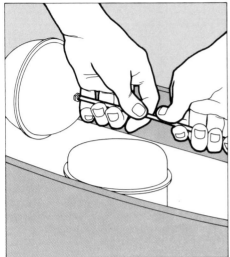

Bending the float arm. If you have a ball valve with a metal float arm, it is a simple matter to alter the level to which the cistern refills. Gently bend the arm upwards a little so that the water's surface is higher when the valve is closed. For a lower level bend the arm downwards. About 15 mm from the invert of the overflow is the normal recommended level of water.

An Emergency Ball Float Repair

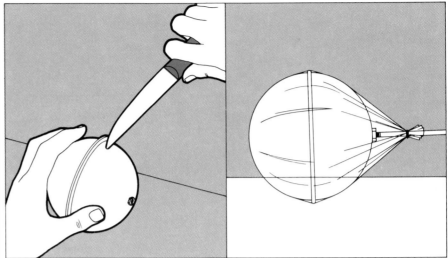

Sealing a punctured ball float. If a ball float springs a leak it will lose its buoyancy and fail to close the valve, leaving the cistern to overflow. For an easy but strictly temporary repair, tie up the float arm, then remove the float by unscrewing it. Enlarge the hole (*above*) and tip out the water. Replace the float and shroud it with a plastic bag tied with string or a rubber band.

Replacing the W.C. Seat

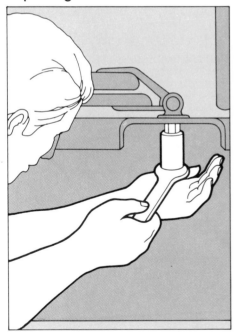

Removing the seat bolts. The two bolts that hold the seat to the pan usually have smooth, rounded heads that provide no grip. They must be removed by unscrewing the nuts beneath the top edge of the W.C. pan. If long-nosed pliers will not loosen them, try a socket spanner with a deep socket. If the bolts are so corroded that you still cannot undo them, try the method on the right.

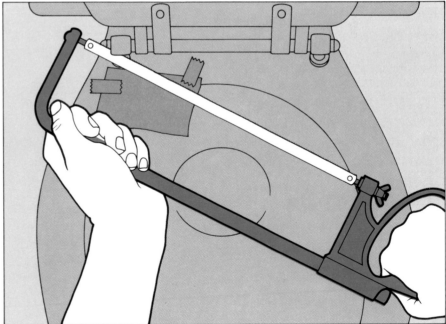

Freeing corroded bolts. Soak intractably corroded bolts with penetrating oil for 30 minutes or even overnight, then try loosening the nuts once more. Do not use force; the brittle china bowl cracks easily. If penetrating oil does not free the nuts, use a hacksaw to cut off the bolt heads, sawing through their washers. Stick cardboard between blade and bowl to protect the china.

A New Look for Flawed Ceramic

The pretty parts of the plumbing system—ceramic tiles, soap dishes and towel rails, and the porcelainized surfaces of fixtures—need repairs as much as the pipes. Gleaming chrome dulls with layers of mineral deposits; ceramic or porcelain enamel is discoloured by rust stains—usually because of a dripping tap that should have been repaired—or by chemicals in water. A heavy object slips from your hand—and you have a chipped bath. Ceramic tiles may even loosen and fall from the wall because of poor installation or the cumulative effects of time and humidity. And one of the most common bathroom repairs—sealing cracks in the joint between the bath and the wall—is a repetitive chore because of changes in the weight of the bath as it is filled with water and emptied again and again.

The chart and instructions on the following pages provide solutions for these problems. In some situations you may have to combine two techniques to get a job done. On page 49, for example, you will find instructions for replacing a broken towel rail. If it turns out that the mounting plate for the new rail does not cover the scar left by the old one, modify the instructions: replace the tile by the technique shown opposite, then mount the towel rail on the new tile by the technique on page 49, Steps 2 and 3.

Whatever job you tackle, take practical precautions. Wear goggles when you shatter a tile; wear rubber gloves when you work with powerful cleansers. And when surrounded by the brittle surfaces of a bathroom, handle heavy tools with special care and attention—a single slip can add a new repair job.

Cleaning Tiles and Fixtures

Problem	Solution
Tile adhesive on surface of tile	Wipe it off quickly with a damp cloth. If it has set, scrape it off carefully with a razor blade or window scraper—without scratching the tile—and then wash the tile with paint thinner. Take special care when handling thinners near plastics.
Dirty seams between tiles Cloudy, filmy tiles	Wash with a toothbrush and detergent. Remove film with a mild detergent and rinse in cold water. Dry with a clean, soft cloth.
Rough, grainy surface on tiles or enamelled baths from lime deposits in hard water.	Dissolve lime deposits on enamelled baths by washing with vinegar. Use dilute lemon juice on plastic baths.
Discoloured enamelled bath	To improve the appearance of an enamelled bath, use a mixture of cream of tartar and peroxide. Stir in enough peroxide to make a paste and scrub vigorously with a small stiff brush.
Soiled or discoloured W.C. pan	Flush to wet the sides of the pan, then sprinkle W.C. cleaner or chlorine bleach on the wet surfaces. Let it stand for a few minutes, then brush with a long-handled W.C. brush and flush. Never try to strengthen the cleanser with chlorine bleach or add ammonia to either: the mixture will cause a chemical reaction to release toxic gases.
Dirty or sticky chromium-plated taps	Wash with a mild soap or detergent and polish with a dry, clean cloth. Use vinegar to remove mineral deposits. Do not use metal polishes and cleaning powders: they will damage the plating.
Iron rust stains on basins or baths	If the fixture is lightly stained, rub with a cut lemon. If seriously stained, use a 5 per cent solution of oxalic acid or 10 per cent hydrochloric acid. Apply with a cloth, leave on only a second and wash off thoroughly. Repeat if necessary.
Green copper stains on sinks or baths	Wash with a strong solution of soapsuds and ammonia. If the stain persists, try a 5 per cent solution of oxalic acid, as above.

Replacing a Ceramic Tile

1 Removing the tile. Using a hammer and cold chisel and wearing goggles, smash the centre of the tile, then prise out the pieces. If a tile falls out in one piece and can be re-used, scrape away the cement on its back. Remove loose or uneven cement from the tile bed.

2 Resetting the tile. Apply the adhesive to the back of the tile and set it into place so that it is even with the adjacent tiles. If the tile does not have spacer lugs on two sides, place toothpicks or spent matchsticks in the joint to space it. Leave the tile to dry overnight.

3 Applying the grout. Use tile grout to fill the spaces round the new tile. Force the grout into the spaces with a fingertip, then use a damp cloth to remove any surplus grout that may have smeared the neighbouring tiles.

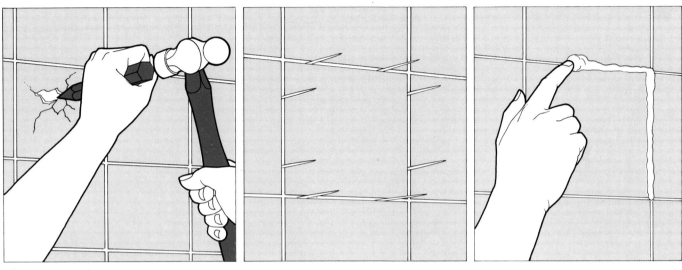

Shaping a Tile to Fit

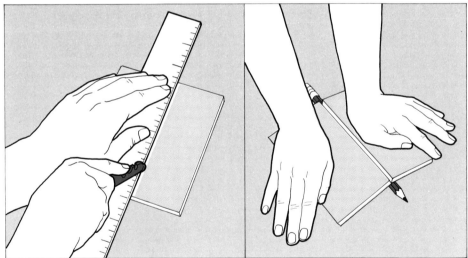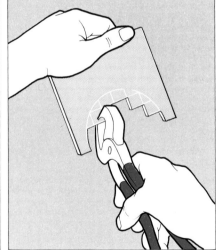

A straight cut. If a tile must be cut to fit into a narrow rectangular space alongside a fixture, outline the part to be removed with a grease pencil. Score the line with a glass or tile cutter; press firmly on the cutter and pull it along the pencil line with a smooth motion *(above, left)*. To break the scored tile in two, place a pencil on a flat surface and position the scored line of the tile over the pencil. Press down equally on both sides of the line until the tile snaps *(above, right)*.

A curve cut. To fit a tile to a curved fixture, outline the excess part of the tile in grease pencil, and with a glass cutter score a grid over the area to be removed. Using pliers or tile nippers, chip away the area. File the edges smooth.

Sealing the Gap
Between Wall and Bath

Caulking the joint. The simplest way to fill the gap between wall and bath is with flexible water-proof caulking compound. Cut the nozzle of the tube at a slight angle and slowly squeeze the compound along the gap, using as steady and continuous a motion as possible. Wait at least 24 hours before using the bath.

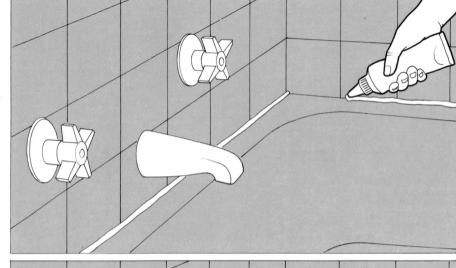

Edging tiles. If caulking will not stay in the wall-bath joint, apply quarter-round ceramic edging tiles, which are available in kits. These tiles are easily attached round the entire rim of the bath with a caulking compound.

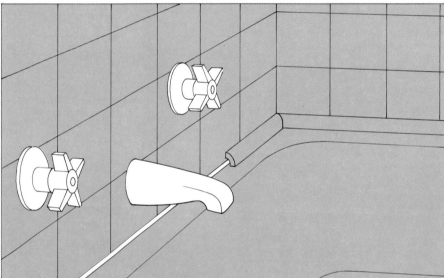

Repairing chipped enamel. Chips on a bath or basin can be covered by building up thin coats of epoxy paint, available in touch-up kits in many colours. Clean the chipped area with white spirit. Then mix a small amount of the paint and hardener in a container. Apply the paint in several coats with a tiny brush, blending it in towards the edges of the chip. Allow the paint to dry for one hour between each coat.

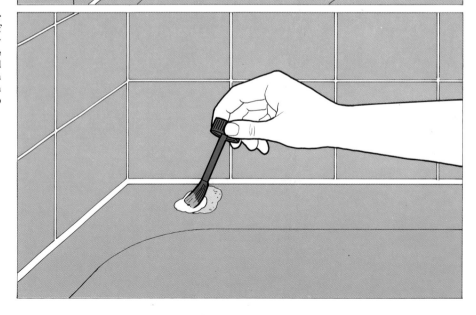

Ceramic Accessories

Broken soap dishes, towel rails and hand rails are replaceable—but as a rule should not be replaced by an identical fitting. In most cases, it is easier to use one that is attached differently.

Most accessories are originally set into tile walls with Portland cement, which is messy to handle. It is therefore best to replace a hand or towel rail with a type that can be screwed to the wall. A light soap dish can be simply attached to the wall with a tile adhesive; select one without a grab handle, so that you will not be tempted to pull yourself up on it.

Replacing a Soap Dish

1 Removing the dish from the wall. With a utility knife, score the grout round the soap dish. Protect the adjacent tiles by covering their edges with masking tape. Then, wearing goggles, lightly hammer the broken parts of the dish to loosen them. Set a cold chisel in the groove made by the knife and tap the chisel to force out the dish. Remove the old grout and adhesive.

2 Replacing the dish. Select a replacement dish that will take up exactly the same number of tile spaces as the old one. Attach the replacement by applying a coat of tile adhesive to the back of the soap dish, then hold it in place with masking tape until the adhesive sets. Wait at least 24 hours for the cement to dry thoroughly, then seal the joints with grout.

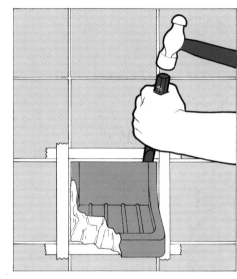
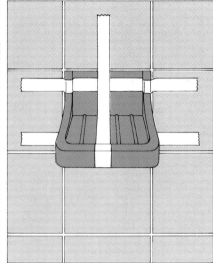

Replacing a Hand or Towel Rail

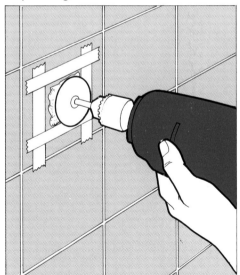
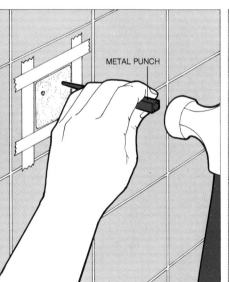
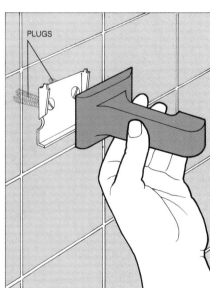

1 Removing the old accessory. If a hand or towel rail breaks, do not gouge out the cement or remaining ceramic piece, but try to get it as flush as possible with surrounding tiles. Protect the tile with masking tape, and, wearing goggles, use a hammer and cold chisel. Then, wearing a face mask, use the sanding attachment on an electric drill. At the edges of the tape, sand the surface by hand.

2 Drilling through tile. Position the plate for your new rail so that it conceals the old cement bed. Use a metal punch and hammer to knock small chips off the surface of the tile so that the drill bit will not skid, then drill the screw holes for the plate with a masonry bit.

3 Fastening the mounting plate. Most modern bathroom accessories have plates that are attached to the wall with screws and concealed by the final assembly. If the tile is set in Portland cement, insert plastic or fibre plugs for the mounting plate screws *(above)*; if you are fastening the unit to a hollow wall, use collapsible anchors. Complete the assembly according to the manufacturer's instructions.

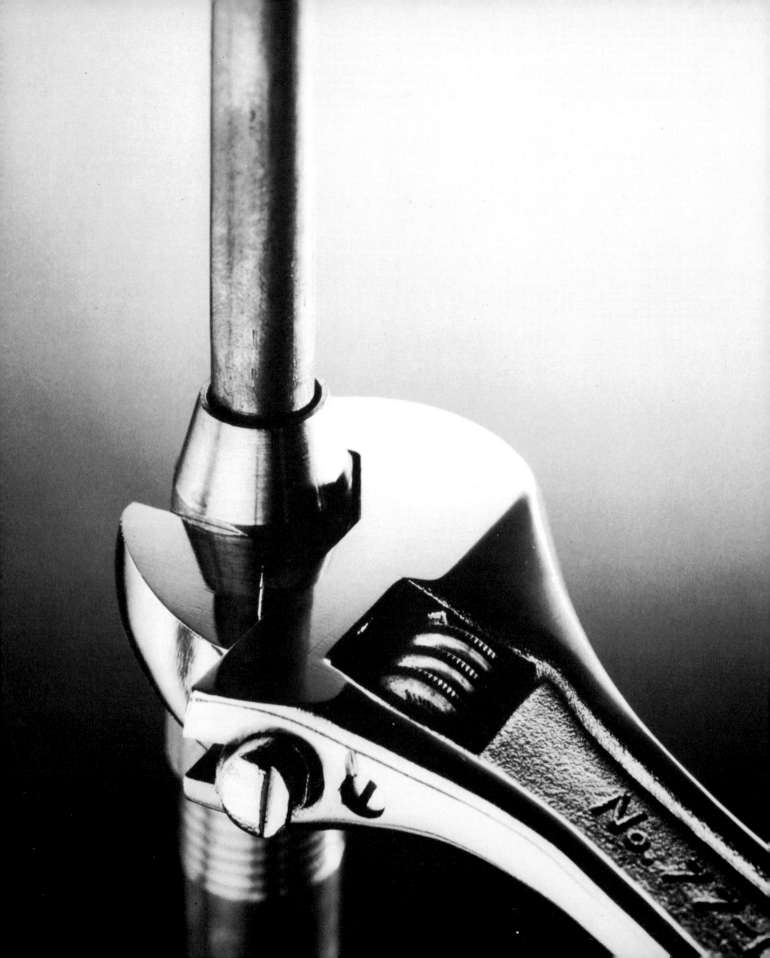

Working with Pipe

Making compression fittings. Copper pipe—the commonest type of water supply pipe—is joined most quickly and conveniently with screw compression fittings, which come in a variety of shapes for different purposes. A threaded nut, slipped over the end of the pipe and screwed to the body of the fitting with the aid of a spanner, makes a watertight seal by compressing an internal ring or "olive" round the tube end.

It is not often that you are forced to cut out a section of pipe and insert a new length—only on that rare occasion when a supply line freezes and bursts, a joint springs a leak or a drain becomes permanently blocked. More often you may decide you want to add an entirely new branch of piping as changing family needs demand additional fixtures and appliances. But whether from choice or necessity, the job is easier than you may think, for modern materials and easy-to-master professional techniques make these chores less daunting than they at first appear.

New materials have revolutionized plumbing. No matter what kind of piping you already have—copper, steel, cast iron, plastic or lead—you can generally make a choice among several materials to use for a repair or a new branch, since there is an array of adapter fittings *(page 53)* that allows any one type to be joined to almost any other. Make the job as simple as possible by selecting the easiest pipe materials to use for the job at hand. For waste pipes and some cold water supply lines, this usually means using plastic pipe, which is quickly cut with a saw and easily welded with solvent cement. An attractive alternative for almost any plumbing job is copper piping, which resists corrosion and is very strong. It is not difficult to cut and handle, and is available in several grades to suit different applications. One of the strongest ways of jointing copper pipe is by soldering *(pages 56–57)*, but compression fittings *(opposite and pages 55–56)* are easier to use and ideal for situations where working with a blow torch is impractical or dangerous.

Even when you are repairing existing piping, there is no need to use the same material for replacement lengths—always provided that the piping you choose complies with local building regulations and water authority by-laws. Cast-iron drainage stacks, for example, are best replaced when cracked or rusted with light, easily handled plastic pipes. However, copper should not be used together with any galvanized pipe; the two metals may create an electrolytic action that will eventually destroy the zinc galvanizing.

Whatever pipe material you choose, the job will go more easily if you follow a procedure used by professional plumbers: complete as much of the assembly as possible at your workbench. Even longer runs of pipe can be partially fabricated there, section by section, then brought to the place where they are to be installed. This method allows you to do much of the task in a well-lit, comfortable work area instead of the dark, cramped places where pipes must sometimes be run. If you prefer soldered joints, it also reduces the amount of soldering that must be done near the inflammable structure of the house and its wiring.

A Range of Materials and Fittings for Every Task

The word plumbing comes from the Latin for lead, and there are still a fair number of lead pipes and fittings around. But today a variety of materials is used in house plumbing—copper, cast iron, steel, brass and plastic. Several are likely to be combined in a house, for each brings a balance of benefits in economy, durability and convenience that makes it the choice for a particular job. And the combination cannot be willy-nilly, for some materials cannot join others without special precautions.

Copper, most popular for supply pipes, but also used for wastes and vents, is convenient to work with and very durable. It is available in straight, 3 metre or 6 metre lengths, either as hard-drawn, thin-walled piping (the most economical type when it it not necessary to bend the tubes) or as half-hard piping that can be bent with the help of special tools. Twenty metre coils of fully annealed flexible tubing in dead-soft temper can also be bought, but piping of this kind is expensive and mostly used for mini-bore central heating systems and for underground lines.

Plastic pipe has become increasingly popular in recent years because it is light, inexpensive and easy to join. Several different plastics are made into pipe. PVC (poly vinyl chloride) is the most usual, either in its unplasticized form (uPVC or rigid vinyl) or plasticized (cPVC). The plasticized form is semi-rigid and able to tolerate the intermittent high temperatures of waste pipes. PVC is not strong enough to be used for high-pressure water supply, and because it softens and distorts when heated it is not suitable for hot water supply. It is easily joined with solvent cement or with integral ring-seal joints that simply push together. Pipes made from polythene, a material flexible enough not to burst if the water inside freezes, are connected with compression-type fittings, and are usually used only for outdoor cold-water supply lines.

Galvanized steel is the strongest plumbing material available for water supply pipes and is preferred for piping exposed to damage. It is heavy, and must be joined with threaded fittings. You may be able to find a plumbers' merchant who will cut the lengths you need and thread them.

Cast-iron pipe is used only for soil pipes, vents and drains. It is joined with bolted mechanical couplings or, common on old pipes, special lead-caulked joints.

The practical considerations of convenience, cost and durability, however, are not the only factors determining the choice of material. The by-laws and building regulations for your area may force decisions. Some prohibit a material in one part of a plumbing system but not another, and may even dictate the method you use to join it. Check with your local authority before investing in your materials.

Metric copper piping is sized by external diameter in millimetres; all other types are sized by internal diameter. When replacing a section, measure its diameter with a ruler and get new pipe of the same size. If you are adding a supply pipe, use the size specified by the manufacturer of the appliance. Choose a waste-pipe size according to the requirements of your local authority: a longer run of pipe needs a larger diameter to ensure satisfactory drainage.

In addition to piping, you also need fittings to join it. A fitting is necessary when piping branches off, changes diameter, joins another type, or, in the case of rigid materials, changes direction. The most common fittings are shown on the opposite page. The shapes are common to all piping—the only difference is the way in which they are joined. You can easily join imperial-sized pipes to modern metric pipes by using special adapter fittings.

Special care must be taken when you are using a fitting to join copper pipe to steel: this should only be done if the water is of a hard nature and problems of electrolytic action have not previously been encountered in the area.

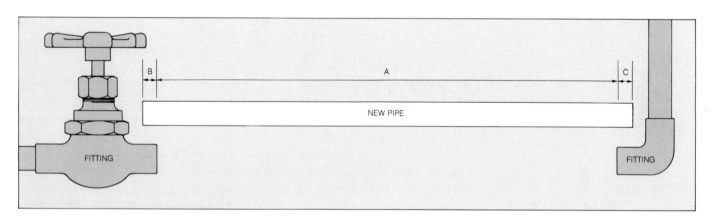

How much pipe do you need? To find out how long a piece of pipe you need between two existing fittings, measure the distance between the faces of the two (distance A). Then measure the distance that the new pipe will extend into each fitting (distances B and C), and add both to the first. If only one fitting is in place, mark where the second fitting will be placed and have someone hold it there while you measure.

Four Categories of Connectors

Branches and turns. An elbow takes rigid piping around a curve; various angles are available up to 180 degrees. A "T" provides a connection for a new branch at its base. A "Y" is a variation of the T usually found in drainage and vent lines to allow pipes from individual fixtures to be joined to one main stack. The branch of a Y can also be plugged for use as a cleaning eye.

Fittings for in-line joints. When two pipes must be connected together in a straight run, a coupling, or sleeve, is used to join them, A nipple, threaded on both ends, extends a coupling for steel pipes. A reducer attaches a length of small-diameter pipe to a larger one. Ts, elbows and Ys, shown on the left, are available with a reducer.

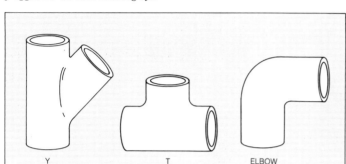

Y   T   ELBOW

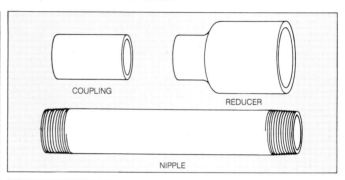

COUPLING   REDUCER

NIPPLE

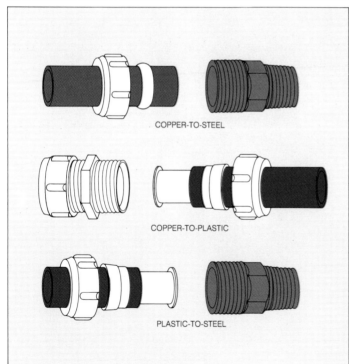

COPPER-TO-STEEL

COPPER-TO-PLASTIC

PLASTIC-TO-STEEL

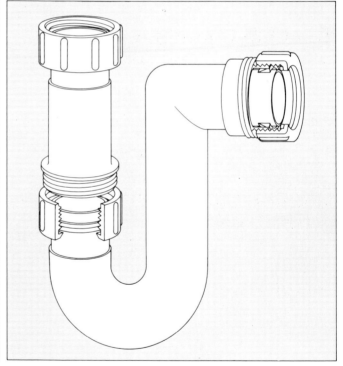

Transition fittings. To connect one type of pipe material to another, a special fitting will fasten both materials firmly. (However, electrolytic action can occur, causing corrosion between dissimilar metals.) The copper-to-steel fitting has a compression fitting at one end, and the other end threaded for steel piping. The copper-to-plastic fitting has a compression joint at each end: one takes the copper pipe and the other has a copper insert to take plastic pipe *(page 59)*. The plastic-to-steel fitting has a compression fitting similarly adapted for plastic, and a threaded end designed to fit on to a steel pipe.

Drainage fittings. The trap, the one fitting used only in the drainage system, keeps a barrier of water in its U-turn to seal out smells from sewers. Traps may be of plastic *(above)* or metal. They may fit together with threaded nuts as shown, or with a push-fit joint containing an integral rubber sealing ring or flange. Since waste pipes depend on gravity to pull waste through the drainage system, their outlets are always angled downwards.

Copper Piping

The techniques for joining copper piping and fittings are the same for adding new runs or repairing damage in old ones. The first step is to cut the pipe square, then clean the mating surfaces of pipe and fitting of burrs. Copper piping can be cut with a pipe cutter or a hacksaw. You can make gentle bends in pipe with a pipe-bending spring (*right, centre*). For joining piping to domestic appliances, it is easier to use flexible connectors—corrugated copper sections that may be bent with the hands (*right, below*).

Joints made with solder, known as capillary joints (*page 57*), are stronger and more leak-resistant than mechanical connections. When soldering, use non-corrosive flux and, for most jobs, Tinman solder which has a 50:50 tin–lead content. Do not use solder with an acid core. If you use fittings manufactured with an integral solder ring, you will not need solder; apply flux, assemble the fitting with the pipes and apply heat from a blow torch until the solder appears at the mouth of the joint.

Before working on plumbing systems with a blow torch, drain the pipes to avoid a dangerous build-up of steam. Place a fireproof mat between the pipe and surfaces that might ignite. Because of the fire hazard, avoid soldering in cramped spaces; use mechanical connectors instead.

Joints made by screwing fittings together are known generically as compression joints, and they come in two kinds: manipulative, which require a special tool (*page 56*), and non-manipulative, which only require spanners (*opposite*). In manipulative joints, the end of one of the two lengths of pipe to be joined is flared slightly to form a watertight socket for fitting. An equivalent effect is achieved in non-manipulative joints by pressure exerted on a compression ring as the nut is screwed home. As the nut is tightened, the edges of the ring are forced into the pipe to indent it slightly and make a double seal.

Compression fittings are available in numerous forms, from simple straight connectors through many types of bend to multiple junctions, valves and taps. They must be made of copper or a suitable corrosion-resistant alloy—usually brass or, for areas with highly acidic water, gunmetal.

Using a pipe cutter. Slide the cutter on to the pipe and turn the knob clockwise until the cutting wheel makes contact with the pipe wall. Turn the cutter once around, tighten the knob a quarter turn, and continue turning and retightening until the pipe is severed. Use the triangular blade attached to the cutter to ream out the burr inside. If you use a hacksaw, remove the inner burr with a round file and any burrs on the end and outside with a flat file or sanding paper.

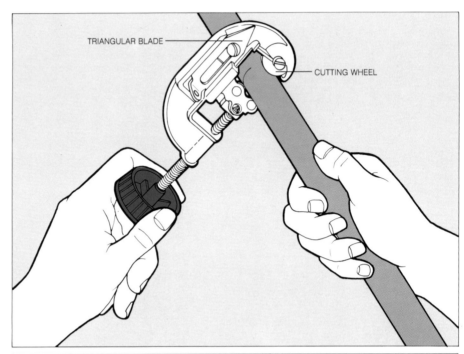

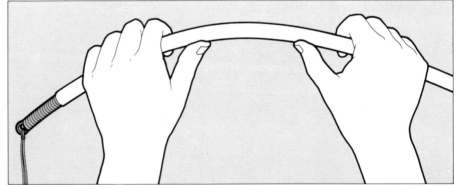

Using a pipe bender. Half-hard copper pipe can be bent by using a pipe-bending spring, to prevent kinks and flattening of the pipe. Slip the bender—matched to the bore and type of pipe—inside the section, using a clockwise twisting motion. Bend the pipe with your hands or form it over your knee. Overbend the pipe a bit, then ease it back to the angle you want. Twist the spring anticlockwise and pull it out of the pipe.

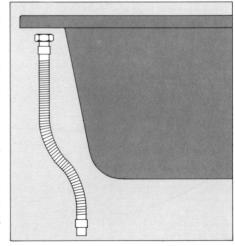

Using a flexible connector. When the alignment of a pipe has to be altered to fit an appliance accurately, the easiest way is to use a corrugated connector that can be bent by hand and attached with compression or capillary fittings at each end. Remember that once the connector has been bent, it cannot be reshaped without the danger of overworking the metal and causing fractures.

Making a Non-Manipulative
Joint with a T-Fitting

1 **Cutting a section from the pipe.** Using a pipe cutter or a hacksaw, remove a section from the existing pipe, long enough to allow the ends of the remaining pipe to reach the pipe-stops inside the T-joint. Deburr the pipe ends with the cutter's blade or with a file and sandpaper.

2 **Applying jointing compound.** Move the pipe ends apart. Slip a compression nut and then a compression ring on to one end of the pipe. To ensure that the joint is watertight, smear jointing compound on the compression ring *(below)*. The jointing compound should not go inside the pipe or on the screw threads of the nut, where it might make the joint difficult to dismantle.

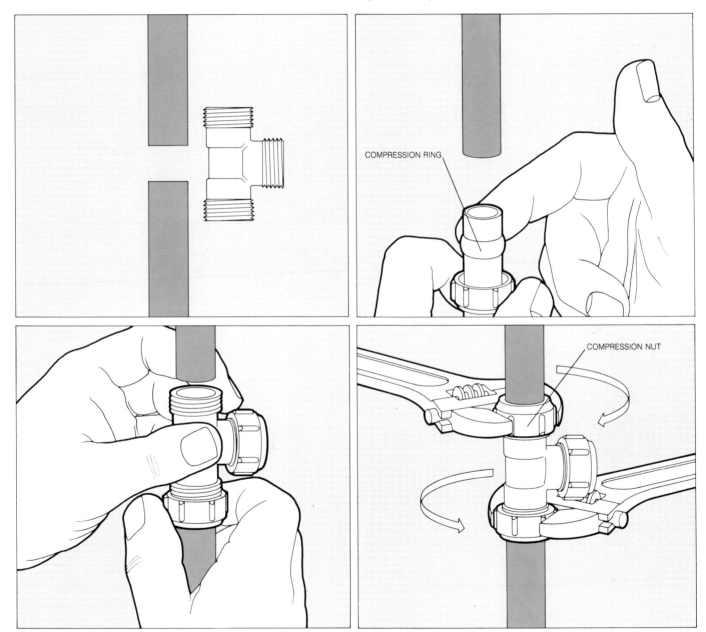

COMPRESSION RING

COMPRESSION NUT

3 **Threading on the fitting.** Slip the body of the T-joint over the compression ring, pushing it on to the pipe as far as it will go. Screw the nut on to the fitting by hand *(above)*. Slip the second compression nut and ring on to the other end, smear the ring with jointing compound and screw the nut on to the fitting.

4 **Tightening the nuts.** With a pair of wrenches or spanners, turn the two nuts carefully in opposing directions. Be careful not to overtighten them, or you may distort the compression rings and cause leaks. A single complete turn of the spanner is enough for most sizes of pipe, and even less for pipes of larger diameter or thin-wall pipes.

A Manipulative Compression Joint

1 **Flaring the pipe.** Slip the compression nut of a manipulative fitting—also known as a Type B fitting—over the end of a square-cut deburred tube. Using a steel drift of the correct size, set the tapered end inside the pipe. Hold the pipe steady and hammer the drift until the pipe end is flared to the shape of the drift. Remove the drift.

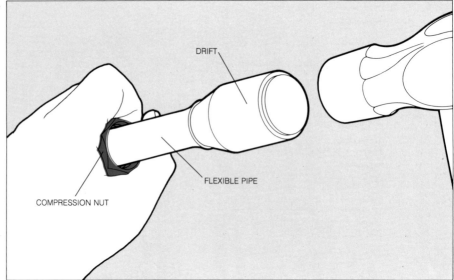

DRIFT

FLEXIBLE PIPE

COMPRESSION NUT

2 **Assembling the joint.** Set the flared end of the tube on to the domed end of the fitting—a straight connector is illustrated, but elbows, Ts and other fittings are also available. Then slide the compression nut up and thread it on to the fitting until it is hand-tight. Finish tightening the nut with a pair of adjustable wrenches, one on the nut and one on the fitting. The other end of the manipulative fitting is joined to a second piece of pipe in the same way. If you wish, smear jointing compound between the mating surfaces.

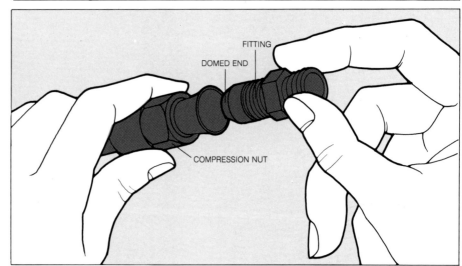

FITTING

DOMED END

COMPRESSION NUT

How to Use a Propane or Butane Torch

The small propane and butane torches generally used to solder copper joints are made in two parts, a combination valve and nozzle assembly, and a replaceable metal tank of fuel. To assemble the torch, simply screw the nozzle assembly to the threaded fitting at the top of the tank. Care should be taken not to "cross" the threads.

To light the torch, strike a match, hold it near the underside of the nozzle and turn the valve slightly anticlockwise. When the torch lights, gradually open the valve further until the flame becomes large enough to heat the area you will work on. Do not open the valve all the way: the flame will not get much larger and the gas pressure will probably blow it out.

When using fixed fuel canisters, hold the torch upright when you are working. If the tank is tilted very much, the liquid gas inside will flow into the valve, blocking it so that the flame goes out.

Such torches are easy and safe to use if they are handled properly. Caution is necessary, however, because the joints to be soldered with the flame are generally to be found near the combustible parts of a house structure.

Before starting to work, cover the area behind the piping with fireproof mats. And make a habit of shutting off the torch whenever you set it aside, even if only for a moment or two—the flame is silent, nearly invisible and easy to forget about.

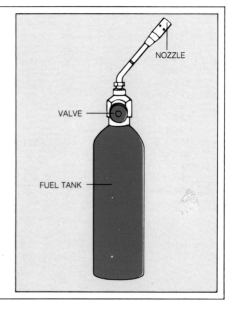

NOZZLE

VALVE

FUEL TANK

Soldering a Joint

1 **Cleaning the copper.** To clean the joint so that melted solder will flow evenly and adhere properly, scour the inner surfaces of fitting sockets with a wire brush. With a piece of emery cloth or steel wool, clean the end of the pipe that will slide into the socket, rubbing until it is burnished bright. When surfaces are cleaned, do not touch them, since even a fingerprint will weaken the joint.

2 **Assembling and heating the joint.** Brush a light coating of flux over the surfaces you have cleaned, assemble the joint and give the pipe a twist to make sure the flux is distributed evenly. Place a fireproof mat behind the joint to protect the surface behind from the flame. Light the torch and play the flame over the fitting and nearby pipe, heating them as evenly as possible. Touch a piece of solder to the fitting and then to the pipe; when the solder melts on contact with both parts, the joint is ready to be soldered. Do not heat further or the flux will burn off and the solder will not flow properly.

3 **Soldering the joint.** Touch the solder tip to the point where the pipe enters the fitting, but do not let the torch flame touch the solder. The solder should melt only on contact with the hot metal; if it does not, take the solder away and continue heating the joint. (Experienced plumbers judge the temperature of a joint so accurately they heat it and remove the torch flame before soldering.) When the joint is properly heated, molten solder is drawn by capillary action into the fitting to seal the connection. Continue feeding solder until the joint is completed. You will need a length of solder equal to the pipe's diameter.

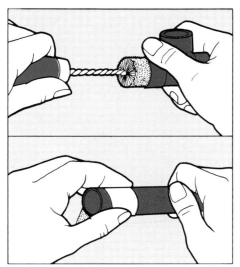

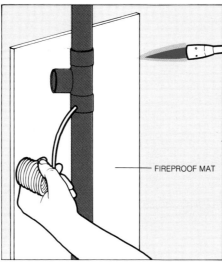

FIREPROOF MAT

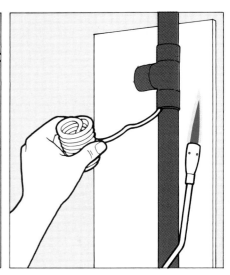

Stopping Leaks in Copper Pipe

Fixing a leaking joint. Leaks in capillary joints are almost always caused by a poor soldering job. Drain the water from the pipe, protect adjacent surfaces with fireproof mats and heat the joint until it can be pulled apart. Take care not to overheat the joint as this will expand the metal and make it difficult to pull apart. Clean the mating surfaces of both pipe and fitting, then apply flux as described for a new joint. Heat pipe and fitting separately, and cover the fluxed surfaces with solder. When both surfaces have been "tinned", scour them smooth with fine steel wool, assemble the joint, and heat and solder it as described for a new joint.

Usually compression joints leak either because of poorly cut pipe or improper assembly. Often a further quarter to half turn of the compression nut in a clockwise direction is all that is required. If this fails, dismantle the joint by loosening the nut, and check to see if the nut and fitting have been cross-threaded. If they have, the entire joint must be replaced. Check that the pipe and compression ring are not bent out of shape. Replace a misshapen compression ring and cut off a distorted pipe end. For a manipulative joint, check the inside of the flared pipe for burrs, gouges or distortions in the flare. To cure any of these problems, cut off the end perfectly square and make a new flare.

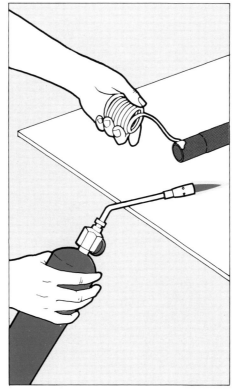

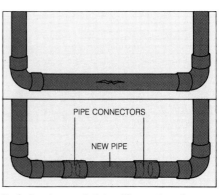

PIPE CONNECTORS

NEW PIPE

Replacing damaged piping. If a section of copper piping is punctured or burst, it can be patched temporarily *(pages 16–17)*, but must eventually be replaced *(above)*. Drain the water from the pipe and cut out the damaged section. Remove only enough pipe to leave undamaged piping with square-cut ends. Replace the section with new piping attached by straight connectors at each end, using soldered or compression joints.

Plastic Piping

One of the main reasons why plastic pipe has become so popular is the ease with which it can be assembled. Rigid pipe and fittings are simply cemented together, and the resulting joint is stronger than the pipe itself. Flexible PVC tubing can be joined with compression fittings similar to the inserts used with copper tube. Transition fittings *(page 53)* make it easy to start a run of plastic pipe from existing pipe of any common material.

Before buying plastic pipe, check your local building regulations. Some areas ban it, while others permit it to be used only outdoors, only for drains or only for cold water supplies. Because of its thermoplasticity, plastic piping is still not a good choice for hot water supplies. Remember that unplasticized plastic pipe (uPVC) should not be subjected to temperatures of more than 65°C. Post-chlorinated plasticized pipe (cPVC) can stand temperatures of up to 85°C, but will soften and expand dramatically when exposed to heat in excess of this. It should be firmly supported with clamps set at 1 metre intervals to offset sagging and set loosely enough to allow the pipe to move slightly.

When using solvents or adhesives, always check that they are compatible with the materials being joined. Assemble rigid plastic pipe only when the air temperature is above 5°C; cold slows the action of the solvent cement, interfering with bonding. Caution: solvent vapours are hazardous. Work in a well-ventilated area, do not smoke, and make sure that there are no naked flames nearby.

Cemented Fittings for Rigid Pipe

1 **Cutting the pipe.** Polythene pipe is soft enough to be cut with a sharp knife or a pair of shears, but cutting rigid or semi-rigid pipe demands precision. A pipe cutter that is used for flexible copper tube is convenient, but it needs a blade meant for plastic. An equally accurate cut can be made with a mitre box and backsaw or a hacksaw with a blade having 32 teeth per 25 mm.

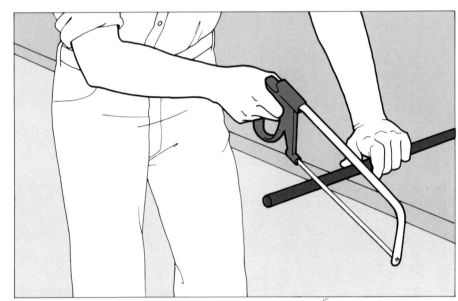

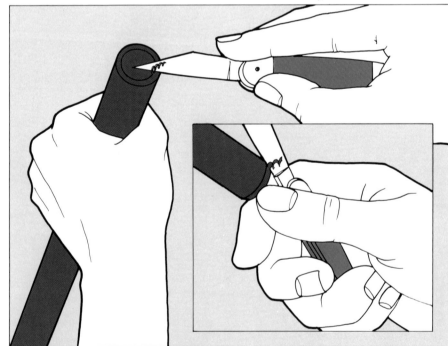

2 **Preparing the pipe end.** Pare away any burrs from the inside of the pipe end. Then bevel the outside of the end so that it will not force the adhesive from the inside of the fitting *(inset)*.

3 **Checking the fit.** With a dry rag, clean the pipe end and fitting of any grease or moisture, then slip the pipe into the fitting: you should be able to push it in half way. If the fit is too tight, the cement may be forced from the joint; too loose and the pipe and fitting may not bond. In either case the joint will leak: try another fitting (size varies slightly). When the fit is correct, adjust pipe and fitting to the position in which they will be set. Mark them so that they can be quickly repositioned after cement has been applied.

4 **Priming and cementing the joint.** Although solvent cement alone generally makes a satisfactory joint, many plumbers prefer to clean and prepare the mating surfaces of the pipe and joint by brushing on a coat of priming solvent. After applying the primer, wait about 15 seconds to allow the surfaces to soften. While the primer is still wet, use a wide brush to apply a thick coat of solvent to the primed surface of the pipe and a thinner coat to the inner surface of the joint. Do not apply so much solvent that it blocks the pipe opening. Immediately slip the pipe into the

fitting, twist the pipe a quarter turn to spread the cement evenly, and align the pipe and fitting to the marks made in Step 3. Delay may cause the joint to fuse in the wrong position. An even bead of glue should appear around the joint. If the bead is incomplete *(below)*, pull the pipe out immediately and apply more cement. When the joint is properly set, hold it in place for 30 seconds, then wait three minutes before starting the next joint. When the job is done, wait at least one hour—or, better still, overnight—before letting water into the new run of pipe.

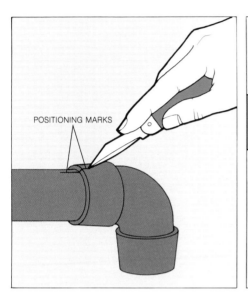

POSITIONING MARKS

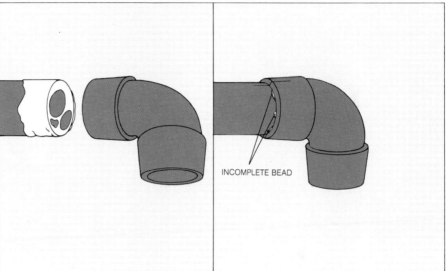

INCOMPLETE BEAD

Making Compression Joints

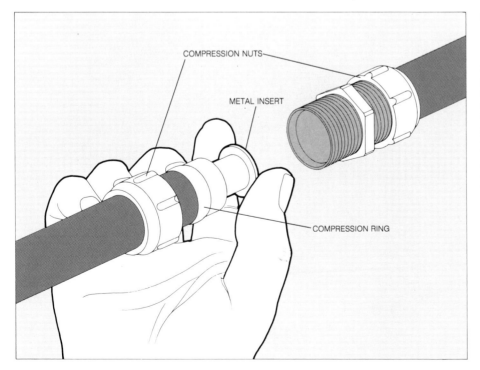

COMPRESSION NUTS

METAL INSERT

COMPRESSION RING

Firm fittings for flexible piping. The flexible plastic piping generally used for cold water supply lines can be joined with metal fittings almost interchangeable with those used for copper piping *(pages 54–55)*. Readily available from do-it-yourself shops, they require no special tools other than saws for cutting and wrenches for tightening. To assemble such a joint, slip a nut and a compression ring over the exposed end of the pipe, then slide the metal insert into the pipe to reinforce it against the pressures exerted when the joint is compressed. Set the pipe end inside the fitting and tighten the compression nuts, at first by hand and then with wrenches.

Steel Piping

Galvanized steel pipe and fittings must be joined with threaded joints or compression couplings. If you plan only a small extension or replacement job, take very careful measurements *(page 52)* and look for an engineering firm or large-sized plumbing and heating suppliers who may be ready to cut and thread the pipe for you. For a more extensive job, use copper or plastic, making connections with adapters, if you cannot get steel pipe to measure.

Threaded joints make assembly easy, but complicate the job of removing a damaged pipe or inserting a new fitting. The problem is that once a pipe or fitting is in the line it cannot be unscrewed as one piece, since loosening it at one end will tighten it at the other. The solution is to cut out the old pipe and install a new one using a fitting called a union *(opposite page, top)*. A simpler device called a slip fitting—a sleeve sealed at both ends by rubber-gasket-fitted compression nuts *(opposite page, bottom)*—can be used to fix a leaking pipe, or in place of a union.

Assembling Threaded Pipe

Applying joint sealers. Before assembling a joint, pipe threads should be covered with one of the three materials shown below to lubricate, seal, rustproof and, if necessary, allow easy dismantling of the joint. Pipe-jointing compound *(below, left)*, the most common material, is spread evenly over the pipe end; use just enough to fill the threads. On water pipes, first wind frump or hemp into the pipe threads *(below, centre)* before applying a thin layer of jointing compound. Plastic joint tape *(below, right)* is even easier to apply. Wind one and a half turns of the tape clockwise over the threads tightly enough for them to show through.

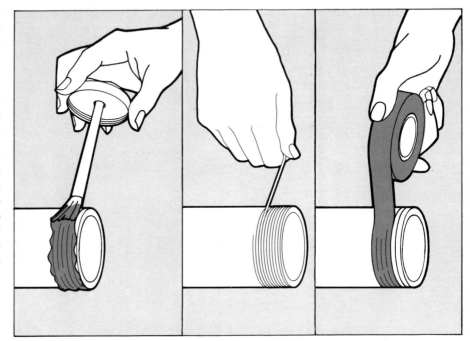

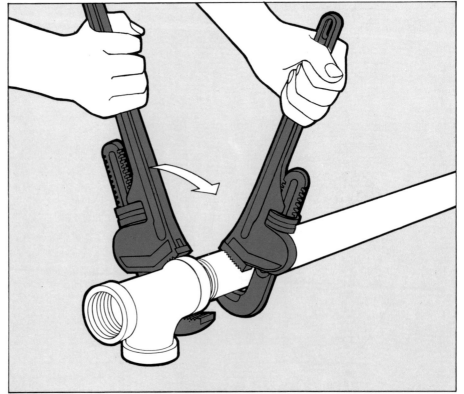

Joining the pipe and fitting. Thread pipe and fitting together by hand to ensure that they are not cross-threaded, then use two pipe wrenches to finish tightening the joint. Turn the fitting with one wrench and hold the pipe steady with the other so that the rest of the pipe branch will not be twisted or strained. The jaws of the wrenches should face the direction in which the force is applied *(arrow)*. Keep tightening until just three threads are visible outside the fitting. Further tightening, which would meet considerable resistance, would strip threads and cause a leak.

Replacing Damaged Pipe with New Pipe and a Union

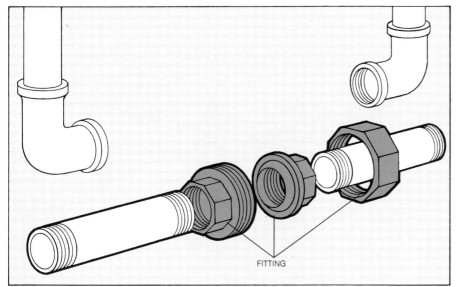

1 **Preparing the parts.** Hacksaw through the damaged section and unscrew each piece of pipe from its fitting by reversing the procedure shown opposite, below. Buy two pieces of pipe and a union whose combined length when assembled will be the same as the old pipe. Prepare the threads of one new piece, slip one union nut on to it and tighten. Slip the ring nut over the end of the second pipe, then thread the other union nut on to the pipe and tighten it.

FITTING

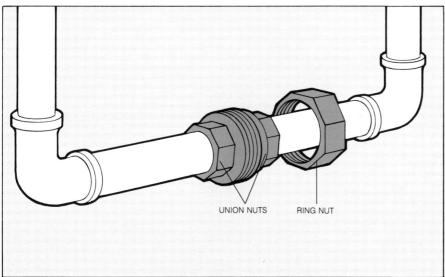

2 **Connecting the union.** Prepare the threads at the end of each pipe section opposite the union nut and screw both sections into the existing fittings. When both sections are tightened, the faces of the union nuts should touch. Smear a small amount of jointing compound on to the mating faces of the union before final assembly. Slide the ring nut to the centre of the union and screw it on the exposed outer threads of the union nut. Tighten it in place with one wrench while bracing the exposed union nut with another.

UNION NUTS   RING NUT

A Sleeve to Stop a Leak

Installing a slip fitting. Cut through the damaged pipe with a hacksaw, pull one cut section aside and slide the fitting on to it. Realign the two sections and slide the fitting over the damaged area. Tighten the nut in place at each end of the fitting. Since this fitting is not as strong as a union, it should be used only on exposed pipe where you can tell if the leak starts up again.

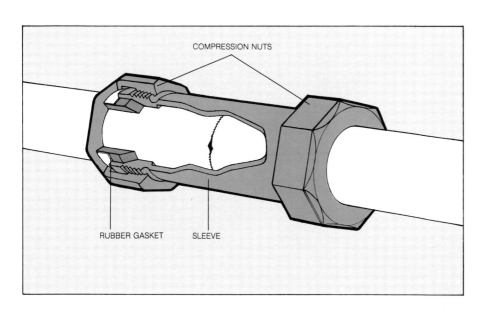

COMPRESSION NUTS

RUBBER GASKET   SLEEVE

Cast-Iron Piping: Old and New

Because of its low cost and durability, cast iron has for a long time been the most popular material for drain, soil and vent pipes, but until recently it was also the most difficult to install because of its weight and the difficulty of joining it. The conventional type, still in wide use, is connected with spigot and socket joints *(page 17)*, which must be sealed with molten lead and a ropelike material called yarn. Plain-ended pipe is easily joined with mechanical couplings *(opposite page)*. It can be inserted into an existing system of spigot and socket pipe to replace a dam-aged section or to add a new one. Leaks at socket joints can often be stopped by using the method shown on page 17.

Three grades of cast-iron pipe are available—medium, heavy and extra heavy. Ask the plumbers' merchant for the weight allowed by your local authority. All grades can be cut either with a saw and chisel *(below, right)* or with a special cutting tool *(below, left)*. Proper support is more important with cast-iron pipe than any other type, both because of its weight and because the mechanical joints are slightly flexible. Use pipe straps or special clamps.

Cutting Cast-Iron Piping

Two ways of working. The easiest way to cut cast-iron pipe is with a link pipe cutter *(below, left)*, usually available from tool-hire firms. If the pipe is already in position, there may not be enough space to cut it in any other way. Wrap the chain section of the tool round the pipe, hook it on to the body of the tool, tighten the knob and work the handle back and forth until the pipe snaps.

Cast-iron pipe can also be cut with a hacksaw and chisel. Mark the circumference of the pipe where you wish to sever it, then support the pipe on a block of wood or a sandbag. With a hacksaw, cut a 2 mm deep groove round the pipe at the mark, then tap round the groove with a hammer and chisel *(below)* until the pieces separate.

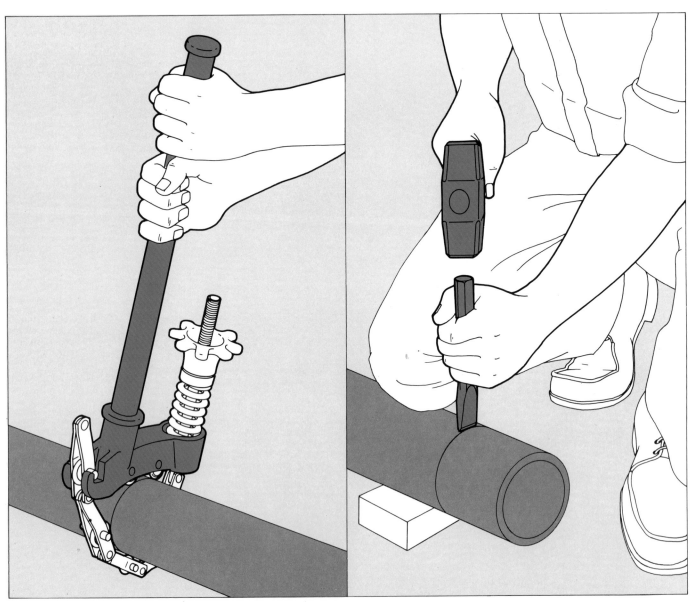

Joining Pipe with Couplings

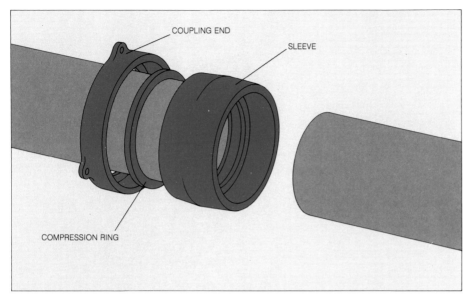

COUPLING END

SLEEVE

COMPRESSION RING

1 **Positioning the sleeve.** Slip one end of a metal coupling over the end of one pipe, then the compression ring and finally the sleeve. If the sleeve has an integral separator ring at its centre, make sure that the end of the pipe butts firmly against it.

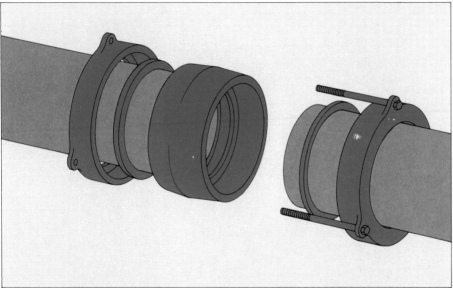

2 **Assembling the joint.** Put the other end of the metal coupling over the second pipe end and add the second compression ring. Insert the bolts through the lugs in the coupling rim and position them as conveniently as possible so that you can tighten them easily when the pipe is in position.

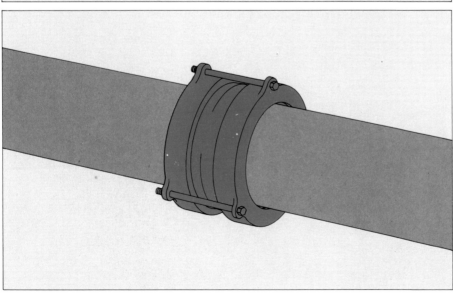

3 **Completing the joint.** Push the end of the second pipe into the sleeve until it butts against the sleeve separator ring. Slide both compression rings up to the sleeve, then slide the two halves of the metal coupling up until they overlap the sleeve. Screw the bolts home into the lugs to tighten and secure the joint.

4

Useful New Installations

Modern fitting for a shower. A single-lever shower mixer valve is simply operated: pull the lever forwards to turn on the water supply, swivel the lever from side to side to adjust the water temperature. Cold water for the shower must be supplied directly from the cold water storage cistern, which must be located at least 1 metre above the shower spray.

New installations both improve and extend the plumbing facilities of the home, bringing them up to date. If you use piping already installed in the house to give yourself a head start, you can achieve the desired results with a minimum of elbow grease and expense. Small jobs may prove as rewarding as big ones. Fitting an outside tap *(page 83)* will result in labour saving for many cleaning and watering chores. Larger projects such as plumbing in a washing machine *(pages 80–82)* or installing a shower unit *(pages 68–73)* may also improve the efficiency of domestic life.

Once you get started, seemingly complicated projects often turn out to be remarkably straightforward. When you replace an old fixture with a new one in the same location, the plumbing connections are simple mechanical fittings; no soldering, threading or cementing need be involved. Replacing a noisy wash-down type W.C. with a stylish and virtually silent new siphonic one *(pages 76–79)*, for example, is largely a matter of loosening nuts with a pipe wrench and removing screws with a screwdriver to take the old cistern off the wall and the old W.C. pan off the floor—and then reversing the process to secure the new close-coupled fixture in place. The chances are that the trickiest part will be lifting the components into position—vitreous china is fragile as well as being heavy, so you will need a helper to manoeuvre the cistern and pan safely.

Wash basins call for even less effort to replace. Ready-made fittings go into place quickly. Wall-mounted wash basins are supported by specially designed brackets packaged with the basins. Should any soldering of the joints be necessary, the use of integral solder-ring fittings makes this the easiest of tasks. Modern vanity-type wash basins are simply set into a waterproof laminate surface or secured with bolts and wing nuts *(pages 74–75)*. Neither kind of wash basin is difficult to install in a room which did not have one originally: a bedroom, a utility room or even a darkroom. It will be necessary to extend the waste and supply lines, but if the distance between the fixture and existing waste service is kept within the recommended maximum length you may not need to install a special trap or vent pipe *(page 67)*. Similarly, the installation of a shower and the plumbing-in of an automatic washing machine are only complicated by the practical considerations of accessibility to existing supplies and wastes.

Before starting any work, familiarize yourself with the layout of the supplies and the drainage, by roughing out on graph paper a diagram of the house and its existing plumbing facilities *(pages 66–67)*. In all modernizing—additions as well as replacements—remember that you need never feel limited by the extent of your present piping. Adapter fittings *(page 53)* make it possible to join new pipes to old ones; and plastic piping may be used to short-cut many of your plumbing projects.

Drawing a Plan of the Pipework

A detailed floor plan of your house, on which are marked the existing water supplies and the drainage services, will help you to determine where you are going to site new plumbing installations. The diagram on this page and the one opposite represent the ground and first-floor plans for a typical semi-detached house, with two living rooms and a kitchen on the ground floor, and a bathroom and three bedrooms on the first.

Extending the water supply pipes to the new fittings should present you with few problems; careful planning will be necessary, though, to ensure that the fittings are correctly plumbed into the drainage system. The diagrams here show the drainage services from the kitchen sink and from the first-floor bathroom. Pipework that is in white indicates where waste pipes would be needed for the addition of a shower in either of the two bedrooms or in the cupboard underneath the stairs; or for the addition of a wash basin—in this case, a vanity unit, which is a basin set into the top of a low cupboard—in the bedroom adjoining the bathroom.

The waste system shown here is the old two-stack variety *(page 12)*, with the bath and basin waste discharging into a hopper head and the W.C. directly into a separate cast-iron soil stack.

When you make the sketch plans of your floors, include the positions of existing plumbing appliances and services, and of possible obstructions to new pipework. Do this plan to scale, adding all the dimensions; you will then be able to tell whether or not the proposed new appliance will fit, and can estimate for materials such as copper piping for extending the supplies, and plastic pipes for the wastes. In new houses, builders' plans are usually available from the agent that negotiated the sale.

Decide on the type of appliance to be added, collect information about its dimensions, choose the optimum position, and lightly sketch in the appliance on your

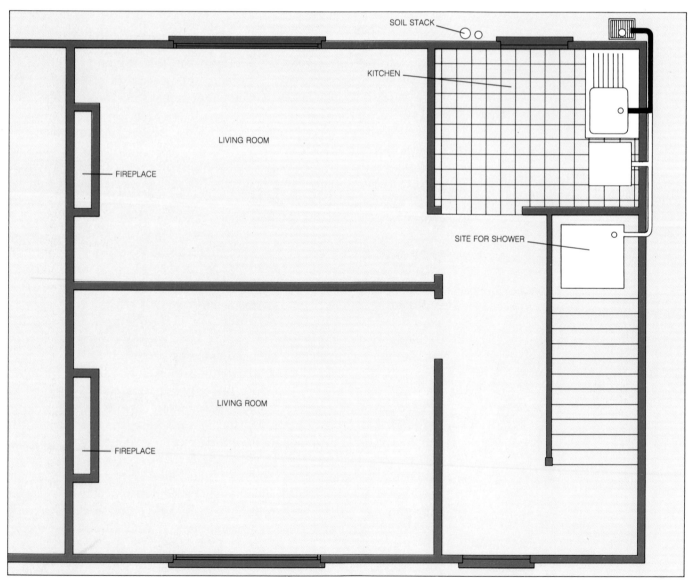

SOIL STACK

KITCHEN

LIVING ROOM

FIREPLACE

SITE FOR SHOWER

LIVING ROOM

FIREPLACE

floor plan. Next, work out the availability of the necessary services. Maybe the water supplies can be extended with only short runs of extra pipe, but you realize that the drain is inaccessible; in that case you will have to work out another position for the appliance. A well-made diagram will readily provide such information.

When designing new plumbing services, try to site the appliance as close as possible to the main stack: long runs of waste pipe are undesirable for many reasons. Blockages are more likely to develop in long runs than in short ones, especially in those that have to change direction in order to by-pass obstructions; noise, created by frictional resistance as water travels through the pipe, may occur; and venting will often be necessary. For example, a 40 mm diameter waste pipe from an installation to a single stack system (combined waste and soil stack) should be vented if its length is more than 2.3 metres.

If you cannot avoid a long run, make sure that you install cleaning eyes at regular intervals and wherever the pipe changes direction. Increase the diameter of the pipe to reduce noise. And if venting is impracticable, you must fix a special re-sealing trap to the appliance. The plan should also allow a sufficient downward gradient of the pipe towards the drainage services. For a 40 mm diameter waste the minimum desirable slope is approximately 1 in 50, that is, 20 mm per metre. If the fall is insufficient, the emptying of waste water from the appliance will be sluggish, again causing blockages. Conversely, if the fall is too great, the appliance will empty too quickly, which may result in the trap seal being removed by differential pressures.

If you have any doubts, make a sketch plan of your project and take it to your local water authority who is very willing to offer help and advice. In any case, the water authority should always be consulted before you embark on any major alterations to the sanitary fittings in the home.

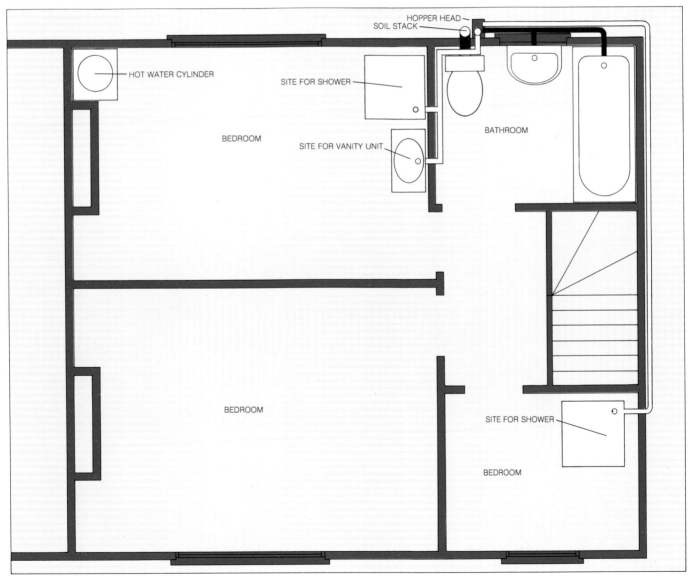

HOPPER HEAD
SOIL STACK
HOT WATER CYLINDER
SITE FOR SHOWER
BEDROOM
SITE FOR VANITY UNIT
BATHROOM
BEDROOM
SITE FOR SHOWER
BEDROOM

Installing a Shower

A purpose-built shower unit offers a convenient and economical way of extending the facilities of a bathroom. Since such showers are self-contained and waterproof and take up less than one square metre of floor space, they can be built into a variety of areas: it could be the corner of a bedroom, a cloakroom, a utility room, or even an empty cupboard under the stairs.

These and the following four pages show you how to install a shower in a corner position. Some experience of home plumbing would be an advantage for this project, and at times you will need a helper. There are five main steps: extending the supplies to the site; mounting the shower tray on to a wooden plinth attached to the floor; extending the waste; installing the metal framework and sliding doors that, together with the walls of the room, make up the shower cubicle; and fitting in place the shower mixer valve that blends the hot and cold supplies, and the sprinkler head attached to this valve.

To comply with water authority by-laws a shower must be supplied with a separate, independent cold supply from the cold water storage cistern. The vertical distance from the bottom of the cistern to the shower outlet must be at least 1 metre; otherwise the water pressure will be insufficient to provide a satisfactory spray.

That apart, the position of the shower will be determined by the proximity of hot water supplies and of waste pipes. Before installing the unit prepare a diagram of existing pipework (page 67).

Extending the supplies to the shower site entails laying new copper piping, which should be firmly supported at regular intervals with pipe-clips. You may be able to run part of the piping beneath floorboards, but some of it will probably have to be bracketed to a wall surface and then boxed in. How you tackle this problem will be determined partly by the site of the shower and partly by your own ingenuity. The exact way in which the supplies are connected to the shower mixer valve will depend, in its turn, on the direction of the extended supply pipes.

The shower area should be well ventilated to prevent condensation. If there is no nearby window it may be advisable to install an extractor fan in the outside wall, or at any rate an air vent.

The finished installation. A two-sided shower unit has been installed in the corner of an upstairs bedroom adjoining the bathroom. The completed unit (below, left) is mounted on a wooden plinth. Each exposed side of the cubicle has one fixed and one sliding panel, while the two interior walls are tiled. A height-adjustable sprinkler head is attached by a flexible metal hose to a mixer valve that both turns the shower on and off and controls its temperature. The boxed-in supplies are behind the tiles in the far corner.

A diagram of existing pipework (below) shows the cold water cistern in its customary position in the loft, where it is fed by the rising main. The cold supplies run from the loft cistern to the bathroom, and directly from the rising main to the kitchen; the hot supplies flow to these rooms from the hot water cylinder, which is situated in the bedroom and has been boxed in. The new shower unit is in the corner formed by an outside wall of the bedroom and the partition wall between the bedroom and the bathroom; it is directly underneath the loft cistern.

To calculate the length of 15 mm copper pipe needed to extend the supplies, first work out the site of the shower mixer valve on the partition wall; it should be 1 to 1.5 metres above the base of the shower tray, which is itself raised some 120 mm above the floor.

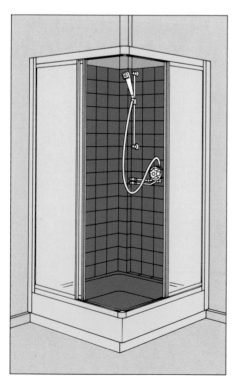

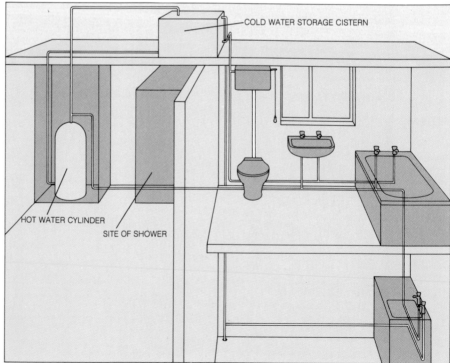

COLD WATER STORAGE CISTERN

HOT WATER CYLINDER

SITE OF SHOWER

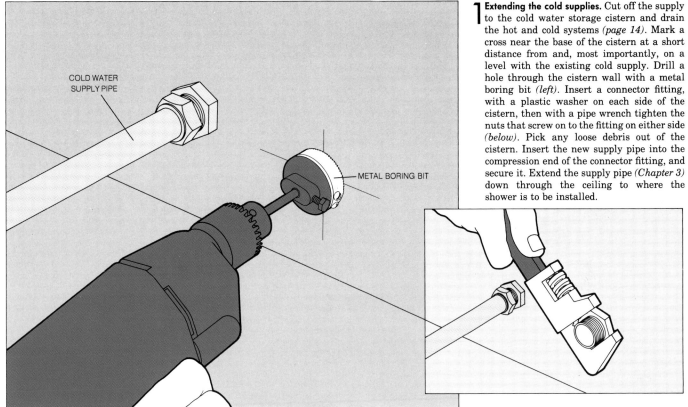

COLD WATER SUPPLY PIPE

METAL BORING BIT

1 Extending the cold supplies. Cut off the supply to the cold water storage cistern and drain the hot and cold systems *(page 14)*. Mark a cross near the base of the cistern at a short distance from and, most importantly, on a level with the existing cold supply. Drill a hole through the cistern wall with a metal boring bit *(left)*. Insert a connector fitting, with a plastic washer on each side of the cistern, then with a pipe wrench tighten the nuts that screw on to the fitting on either side *(below)*. Pick any loose debris out of the cistern. Insert the new supply pipe into the compression end of the connector fitting, and secure it. Extend the supply pipe *(Chapter 3)* down through the ceiling to where the shower is to be installed.

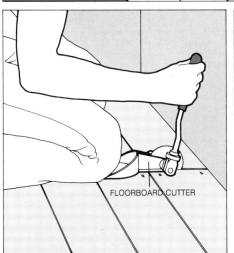

FLOORBOARD CUTTER

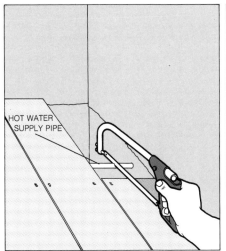

HOT WATER SUPPLY PIPE

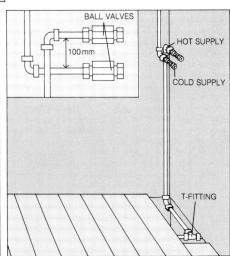

BALL VALVES

100 mm

HOT SUPPLY

COLD SUPPLY

T-FITTING

2 Exposing the hot water supply. Intercept the hot supply at a point near the wall to which the shower valve will be fixed. Using a floorboard cutter—available from plumbers' merchants, tool suppliers or hire shops—saw through the board that conceals the pipe. Make the cut where the board runs over a joist (indicated by a line of nails), so that the section of the board lifted can later be nailed back. Make sure that the cutter is set to the thickness of the board and no more.

Loosen the cut section by working between it and the adjacent floorboard with a broad flooring bolster or cold chisel. Prise it up by hammering home the bolster near the cut end. Remove the section to expose the pipe.

3 Finishing the supply lines. With a hacksaw, sever the pipe in two places to remove a small section *(above)*; the length will depend on that of the 15 mm fitting that will replace it *(page 55)*. Though the hot water system has been drained, it is possible that a small amount of water still trapped in the pipe may be released.

Install the T-fitting with its outlet pointing so that the hot supply can be extended under the floor towards the corner of the room and then, using an elbow fitting, upwards *(above, right)*.

Bring the cold supply down and the hot supply up so that the two vertical pipes overlap by about

100 mm. To each supply attach an elbow fitting (its outlet pointing horizontally towards the site of the shower valve), then a short length of pipe, and finally a ball valve or mini stoptap *(inset)*. Make sure that the valves are in the "off" position. The house's hot and cold supplies can now be restored.

Cut a notch from the wall end of the section of floorboard removed, so that it can fit round the hot supply; then nail the board back in position. Box in the shower supply pipes by means of two wooden battens screwed to the wall and a plywood strip nailed to the battens.

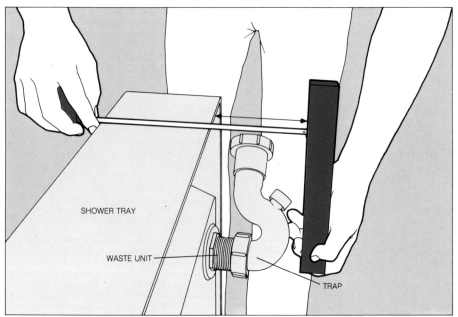

4 **Preparing to install the shower tray.** With the ceramic shower tray on its side, fit the waste unit, securing it on the underside by tightening the retaining nut provided. Screw on the P-trap and then, to determine the height of the plinth needed to raise the tray and waste unit above the floor, hold a straight piece of wood vertically about 30 mm from the bottom of the P-trap *(above)*, and measure the distance between the wood and the bottom of the tray.

5 **Putting the shower tray in position.** With five lengths of 50 mm wood construct a plinth, nailed or screwed together; cut one corner away, and make a removable panel to allow access to the waste *(above)*. The depth of the wood should be equal to the measurement taken in Step 4. The external dimensions of the plinth are slightly less than those of the tray, to allow for a fascia of tiles or other material to be added to its two exposed sides.

Place the plinth in its corner site, then get someone to help you lift the heavy, fragile ceramic tray on top of the plinth *(left)*, its waste in the position indicated. Adjust the P-trap until its outlet faces the partition wall, and mark the wall opposite the outlet. Remove the tray and plinth. With a masonry core drill, or a hammer and chisel, make a hole slightly more than 40 mm through the wall to the bathroom, at the marked position.

Now replace the wooden plinth and nail or screw it to the floor. Replace the shower tray.

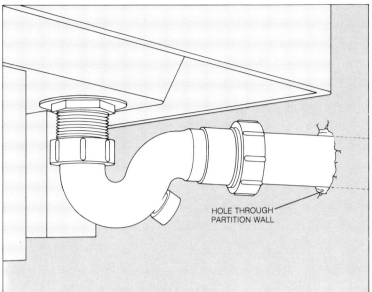

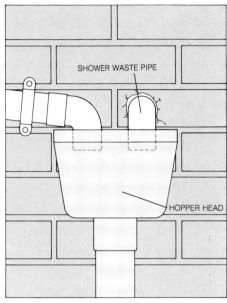

SHOWER WASTE PIPE

HOPPER HEAD

HOLE THROUGH PARTITION WALL

6 **Extending the waste.** Lead the waste through the hole using 40 mm plastic pipe attached to the P-trap with a compression fitting *(above)*. With a sand-and-cement mix, fill the gap between tray and wall. Fix an elbow fitting to the pipe, and with two further lengths of pipe and an elbow fitting take the waste behind the W.C. and above the hopper head of the waste stack.

7 **Completing the waste.** With a masonry core drill, or hammer and chisel, make a hole to take the waste through the wall at this position. To ensure an adequate fall in the waste the hole should be as near to the level of the bathroom floor as possible. Lead the waste through the wall with an elbow fitting, plastic piping, and an elbow fitting pointing into the hopper head.

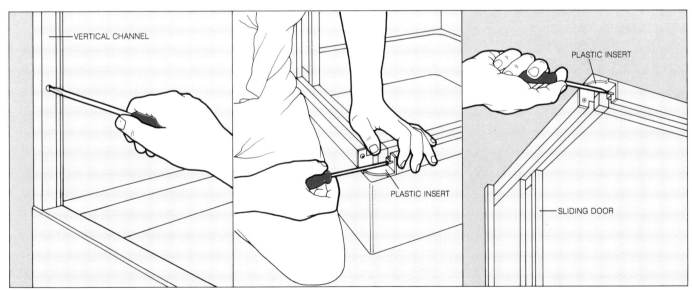

VERTICAL CHANNEL

PLASTIC INSERT

PLASTIC INSERT

SLIDING DOOR

8 **Installing the shower doors.** With screws and plugs, attach to the two walls the two vertical metal channels that will hold firmly in place the fixed glass panels on either side of the cubicle *(above)*. Use a plumbline or spirit level to ensure that the channels are vertical. To bridge the gap between the shower tray and the inner wall, the metal channel on this side must be attached not directly to the wall but to a vertical wooden batten that has itself been screwed to the wall.

The shower's two side units come from the supplier already assembled, each with a fixed and a sliding glass panel, and an upper and a lower metal runner. Spread a layer of mastic along one of the upper edges of the shower tray, then lift one of the side units and place it on the tray, with the fixed glass panel slotted into the metal channel screwed to the wall. You may need help to do this. In the same way install the other unit.

Secure the two units together at the base by interlocking plastic inserts and self-tapping or set screws *(above, centre)*. Similarly secure the side units together where their upper metal runners meet *(above, right)*. With mastic fill any gaps between the completed framework and the ceramic base, and between the framework and the walls.

With waterproof adhesive, tile the interior walls of the cubicle, including the box that hides the supply pipes. Finish off the tile surround with grouting. With tiles or plastic laminate, face the exposed sides of the plinth and the removable panel that allows access to the waste.

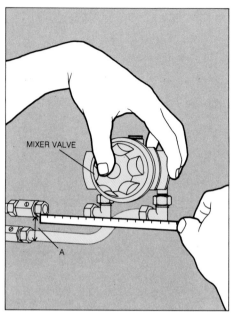

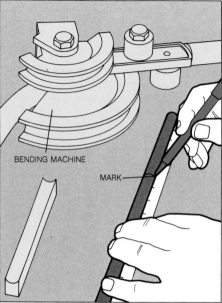

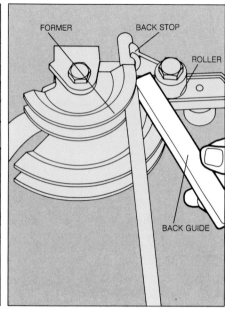

9 **Preparing to install the shower valve.** Hold the valve in place, its elbow fittings in line with the upper (hot) supply pipe. Measure the distance from the hot supply to the valve's left-hand elbow fitting; cut chrome-plated copper pipe to this length. Repeat for the cold supply pipe, allowing for two bends, an extra distance equivalent to A, above.

10 **Marking the first bend.** With a ruler, estimate where the first bend in the cold supply connecting pipe should be, and mark its position with a pen. The bends can be made either with a pipe-bending spring (*page 54*) or a special machine, illustrated above, that is obtainable from hire shops.

11 **Inserting the pipe in the machine.** With the bending machine on its side, insert the pipe until the pen mark just touches the outer edge of the curved former. Locate the pipe end under the back stop to secure it. Position the back guide between the roller and the pipe.

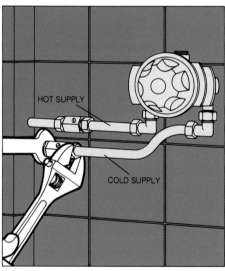

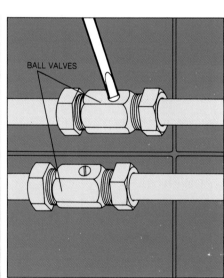

15 **Drilling holes for the shower valve.** To stop the tiles breaking, apply strips of masking tape over the site of the valve. With the valve held in position use a pen to mark where the screw holes are to go, then drill the holes with a masonry bit drill (*above*). Strip off the tape and insert wall plugs.

16 **Installing the shower valve.** Holding the valve in place, fit the two lengths of copper pipe between the ball valves of the supplies and the elbow fittings of the shower valve. Tighten the connections with a spanner (*above*). Screw the shower valve to the wall.

17 **Testing for watertightness.** Test the ball valves by turning them to the "on" position. The exact procedure for doing this will depend on the type of valve you use. Here, a screw on each valve is turned through 90 degrees until the screw slot is parallel to the direction of the supply pipe.

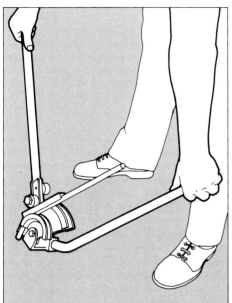

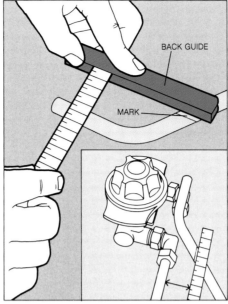

BACK GUIDE

MARK

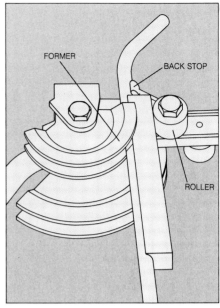

FORMER

BACK STOP

ROLLER

12 **Making the first bend.** Grasp the handles of the bending machine with both hands and firmly pull the handles towards each other. The pressure exerted on the back guide will hold the pipe rigid while a roller mechanism passes over it to make the bend, which should be of about 30 degrees.

13 **Measuring the second bend.** With a ruler and the back guide at right angles to it, position the back guide at distance A from the pipe *(above)* and, with a pen, mark the second bend. The inset diagram shows the pipe placed in position by the shower valve.

14 **Making the second bend.** With its bent end pointing towards the right, insert the pipe into the bending machine so that the pen mark forms a tangent with the outer curved edge of the former *(above)*; ensure that the back stop is located underneath the pipe. Position the back guide and make the second bend of 30 degrees.

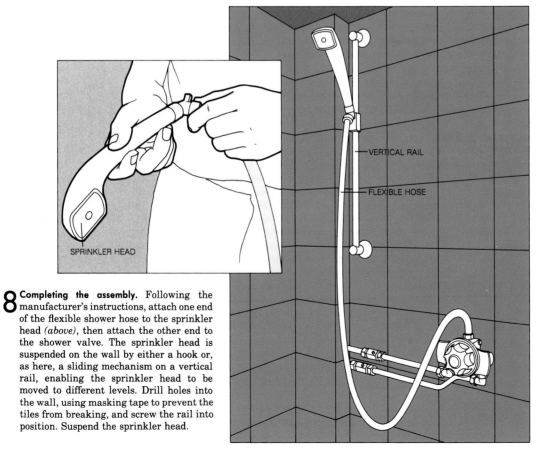

SPRINKLER HEAD

VERTICAL RAIL

FLEXIBLE HOSE

18 **Completing the assembly.** Following the manufacturer's instructions, attach one end of the flexible shower hose to the sprinkler head *(above)*, then attach the other end to the shower valve. The sprinkler head is suspended on the wall by either a hook or, as here, a sliding mechanism on a vertical rail, enabling the sprinkler head to be moved to different levels. Drill holes into the wall, using masking tape to prevent the tiles from breaking, and screw the rail into position. Suspend the sprinkler head.

Connecting a Vanity Unit to Existing Pipes

Taking out a wall-hung or pedestal basin and replacing it with a vanity unit is part plumbing and part carpentry. You will need to disconnect the old basin, cut a hole in the surface of the vanity unit to take the new basin, fit the basin and reconnect the supply pipes.

Before buying the ready-made unit, measure the available space carefully, then choose the counter-top basin to fit the new unit. The plastic basin used in this demonstration has a traditional plug and chain, and hot and cold water taps that are mounted on the left. The taps, basin and cupboard can all be bought separately, but to ensure that the complete unit is compatible it is obviously easier if you buy everything from the same source.

The counter-top basin fits into a hole in the top of the unit; usually the manufacturer supplies a template for cutting the hole. There are several different types of basins: the self-rimmed ones overlap the counter tops and are supported by them; the frame-rimmed model is secured with lugs that connect frame, basin and counter top. The unrimmed recessed basins *(below)* are held by bolts and metal flanges. All must be sealed with mastic.

You will also need a slotted waste connection, an overflow fitting, a suitable trap, and tap connectors to enable the final connection of the water supplies to be made to the taps. Corrugated flexible copper pipes (15 mm) facilitate easy connection of the supplies, especially in awkward places, and are obtainable with tap connectors already attached. Integral ring-type fittings can be used for all joints. They cost slightly more than end-feed fittings but this factor is offset by the ease with which they can be installed: using a blow torch, you need only apply sufficient heat to melt the solder and the joint is complete *(page 57)*.

Removing the old basin. After turning off the water, disconnect the supply pipes. Disconnect any bolts that hold the basin to the top of the pedestal. Lift off the basin. Remove any screws that secure the pedestal to the floor. If there is any plaster of paris under the base, rock the pedestal back and forth to loosen it. If necessary, wrap the base with a towel to keep chips from flying and, wearing goggles, pound with a hammer until the base comes loose. Scour or sand off the plaster remaining on the floor.

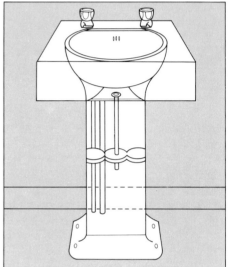

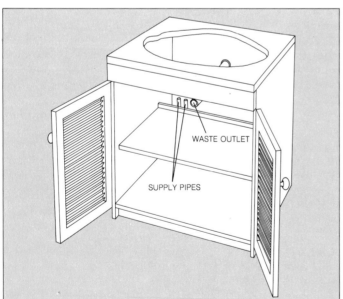

1 **Positioning the cabinet.** After cutting the hole for the sink with a jigsaw, set the cabinet against the wall; the waste outlet should be centred. You may need to adapt the length of the existing hot and cold water pipes; they should terminate above the cabinet's false backing panel so that they are accessible for final connection to the tap tails after the unit has been fixed to the wall.

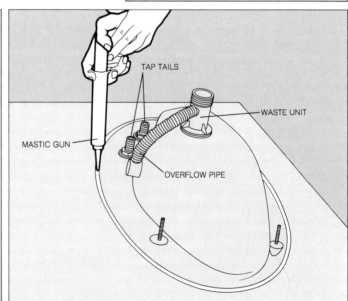

2 **Preparing to fit the basin.** Drop the tap tails through the tap holes in the basin, making sure that hot and cold correspond to the position of the supplies. Tighten the nuts beneath, using a basin wrench. Fit the waste unit and connect it to the overflow pipe *(page 34)*. Turn over the basin and rest it on a sheet of paper on the floor. Use a mastic gun to apply a thin beading of mastic round the under edge of the basin.

3 **Setting in the basin.** Taking care not to touch the edges of the basin, turn it over and lower it into the hole, pressing down firmly until the excess mastic squeezes out. Use a damp cloth to remove mastic from the surround before it dries. Slip the metal flanges on to the bolts. Secure the basin by tightening the wing nuts, forcing the flanges against the underside of the counter top *(inset)*.

4 **Installing a P-trap.** Connect the waste before you connect the water supplies. The plastic P-trap used here swivels from side to side so that small adjustments can be made if the waste is slightly out of line. Hand-tighten the trap *(page 39)*.

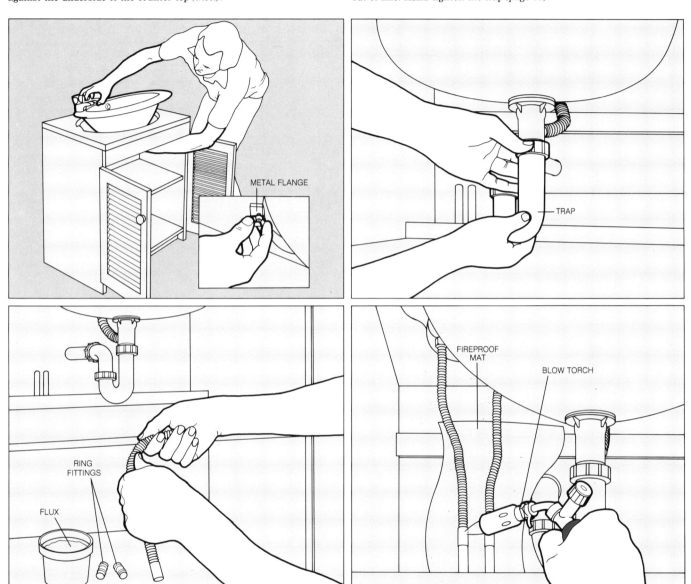

METAL FLANGE

TRAP

RING FITTINGS

FLUX

FIREPROOF MAT

BLOW TORCH

5 **Preparing the connecting pipes.** Corrugated flexible copper bend pipes (with tap connectors attached) are easily bent by hand to connect neatly to the supply pipes by means of integral ring fittings. Use wire wool to clean the free ends of the copper pipes and the supply pipes, and the bore of the two integral ring fittings. Apply flux to the inner surfaces of the fittings, and the outer ends of the pipes to be connected.

6 **Soldering the connections.** Fit the integral ring fittings into position between the supply pipes and the ends of the copper bends. Protect the plastic trap with a fireproof mat. With a blow torch, play heat gently over the fittings and approximately 50 mm of the pipes at either side; when a thin bead of melted solder appears at the mouth at either end of each fitting, the joint is complete. Let the joints cool. While the taps are held firmly in position, tighten the nuts of the tap connectors on to the tap tails with a wrench. To complete the job, turn on the water supply.

Replacing a W.C.

Installing a new W.C. from scratch takes a good deal of plumbing expertise, but replacing a damaged or old-fashioned one with an up-to-date model is a relatively simple job. The new pan fits into the existing soil pipe and often the cistern can be connected to the existing cold water supply pipe.

If you are replacing a high-level cistern with a compact modern W.C. as shown on the following pages, you will need to make a new inlet connection to the supply pipe and conduct an overflow through the wall. Once you have disconnected the old cistern, you have to seal off the open inlet on the supply pipe. Cap it with a special compression or capillary fitting, or, for a neater job, replace the section of supply pipe from just below the ceiling to the connection for the new inlet with new 15 mm copper pipe.

The critical factor is the amount of existing soil pipe that has to be cut off to allow the close-coupled unit to butt against the wall. This is established by a simple measurement (Step 5); if you intend to cover your walls with tiles or wood-cladding before making the final connections, add this thickness to your calculation.

The internal mechanisms of the new cistern are often already installed; if they are not they will be accompanied by instructions for assembly. The necessary washers and hardware for fitting the cistern to the pan will also be included, but you may need to buy 60 mm brass countersunk wood screws for securing the pan to the floor and the cistern to the wall. Place 15 mm tap washers under the heads of the screws before fixing the cistern to the wall.

Buy a plastic push-fit pan connector for the diameter of your soil pipe. Other items needed are 20 mm plastic piping and two elbow joints for the overflow, a compression elbow and T-fitting for the connection with the water supply, and possibly mastic for adjusting the level of the pan.

The job requires few tools: a spanner or pipe wrench, screwdriver, hammer, spirit level, tape measure and, available from hire shops, a link pipe cutter. If you are removing a cemented floor-exiting pan, you will also need a cold chisel.

Have a helper nearby when you remove the old cistern: some are very heavy.

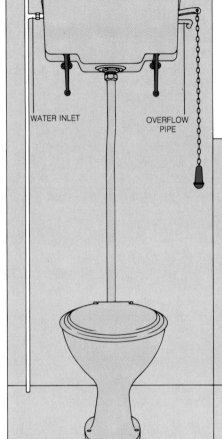

WATER INLET

OVERFLOW PIPE

Old and new W.C.s. On the left is a high-level wash-down W.C. The supply pipe brings water from the storage cistern in the loft or, in the case of direct supplies, straight from the mains. Illustrated below is a close-coupled unit, its cistern mounted on the back of the pan. Modern suites come in many colours, and cistern sizes vary.

OVERFLOW PIPE

WATER INLET

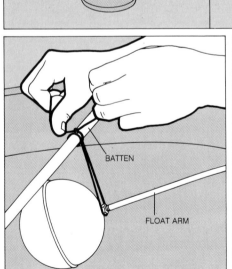

BATTEN

FLOAT ARM

1 Draining the system. Shut off the water supply to the W.C. Remove the lid of the cold water storage cistern, place a batten across and tie the float arm to it (above), to close the float valve. Turn on the cold water taps in the bathroom; when water stops, flush the W.C. The system, excluding any mains supplied tap, is now drained. If the water is from the mains, turn off the cold water stoptap.

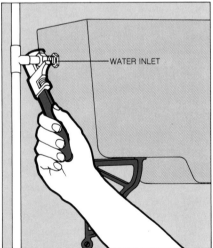

WATER INLET

2 Disconnecting the inlet pipe. Disconnect the inlet pipe to the old cistern. Using a spanner or a pipe wrench, undo the nut that joins the two together (above). If the joint cannot be moved, saw through the pipe with a hacksaw. Cap the open end to the supply or replace the section of supply pipe from just below the ceiling to the point of connection for the new cistern inlet.

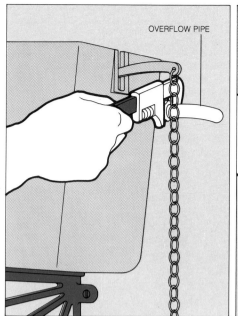

OVERFLOW PIPE

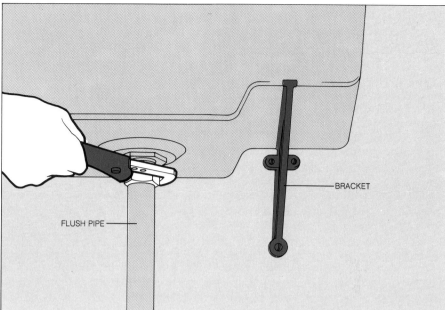

OVERFLOW PIPE

FLUSH PIPE

BRACKET

3 Removing the overflow pipe. Undo the nut that connects the overflow pipe to the cistern. Again, if the nut is stubborn, you will have to saw through the pipe. Pull the pipe from the wall; if necessary, use a hammer and cold chisel to loosen the cement that holds it. Make good the hole.

4 Freeing the flush pipe and cistern. Using either a spanner or a pipe wrench, loosen the nuts at each end of the flush pipe, or simply cut through it at each end. You can now lift the old cistern clear of the brackets. Undo the screws of the two brackets that supported the cistern. If the screws are rusted and impossible to turn, you may have to prise the brackets away from the wall.

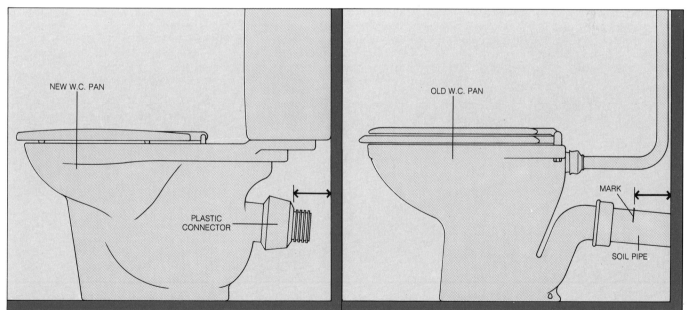

NEW W.C. PAN

PLASTIC CONNECTOR

OLD W.C. PAN

MARK

SOIL PIPE

5 Marking off the soil pipe. Push the wider end of a plastic push-fit connector over the outlet of the replacement pan. Place the new cistern on the back of the pan, and position the assembly against a convenient wall. Measure the distance between the rim of the connector and the wall *(above)*. This is the length of soil pipe needed for the final connection. Remember to add the thick- ness of any wall covering you may apply to your measurement. Remove the connector. Now mark your measurement on the existing soil pipe *(above, right)*. After the old pan has been removed, the soil pipe will be cut off at the mark. The spigot end of the connector will fit inside the cut-off pipe when the new pan and cistern are finally positioned.

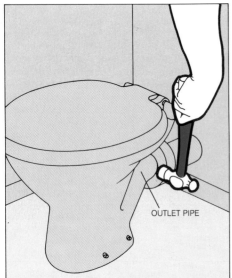

OUTLET PIPE

LINK PIPE CUTTER

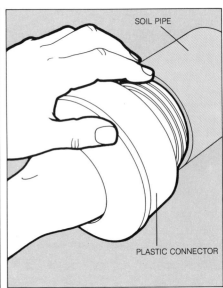

SOIL PIPE

PLASTIC CONNECTOR

6 **Removing the old W.C.** The old W.C. pan can now be removed. Unscrew it from the floor, then sever the outlet pipe of the pan in front of the joint with a sharp blow of a heavy hammer *(above)*. Wear safety goggles. (For floor-exiting pans, see box below.)

7 **Cutting the soil pipe.** Use a link pipe cutter to cut through the soil pipe at the mark you made earlier *(above)*. Clamp the cutter in place and work it back and forth several times until the cast-iron pipe is severed.

8 **Fitting the connector to the soil pipe.** Ease the spigot end of the pan connector into the soil pipe. Hold the pipe steady with one hand, while using the other hand to manipulate the connector from inside. This will ensure that the rim of the socket fits snugly against the end of the soil pipe.

A Vertical Soil Pipe

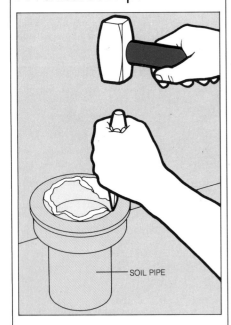

SOIL PIPE

Removing a floor-exiting pan. Sever the vertical outlet pipe *(Step 6, above)*. Remove the pan and stuff a rag into the drain outlet. With a hammer and cold chisel, chip out remaining fragments of the pan. The rag will prevent debris from falling down the drain. (Use the same tools to free the pan if it is cemented to the floor.)

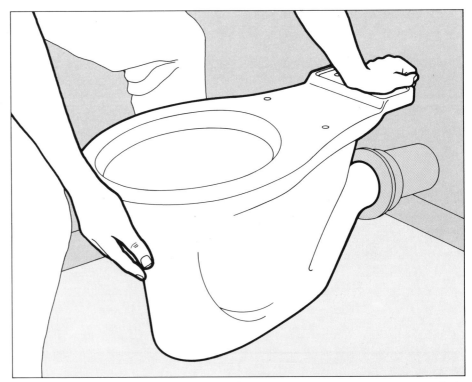

9 **Positioning the new pan.** Align the pan with the open end of the connector and gently push the pan's outlet into the socket as far as it will go. Do not screw the pan to the floor yet.

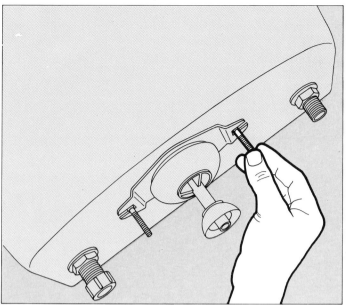

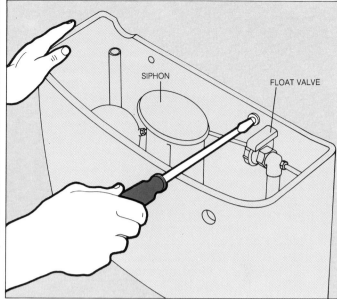

10 **Securing the cistern to the pan.** With the cistern lying on the floor, assemble the fittings on the base of the cistern *(above)* and fit the siphon and valve inside. Follow the manufacturer's instructions. Rest the cistern on the porcelain shelf at the back of the pan and allow the two bolts to drop through the corresponding holes on the shelf. Secure the cistern to the pan using the washers and nuts provided.

11 **Securing the pan and cistern into position.** With a spirit level, check the level of the pan. If it is not level insert a cushion of mastic compound under the rim of the base; press down firmly and evenly on the pan to squeeze out excess compound. Screw the pan to the floor. Through the two holes in the back of the cistern, drill holes in the wall for plugs; then, with 15 mm tap washers under the screw heads, screw the cistern to the wall.

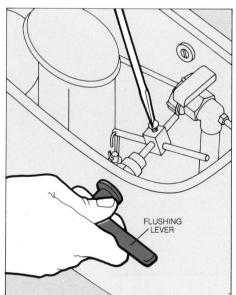

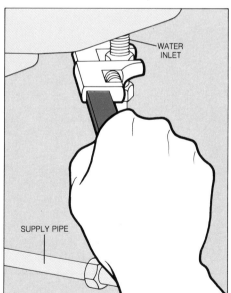

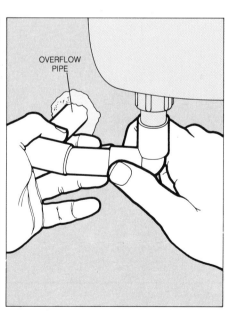

12 **Assembling the flushing lever.** Follow the manufacturer's instructions for assembling the flushing lever mechanism and linking it to the siphon. Adjust the alignment of the flushing arm and lever arm until the flushing action is smooth, then tighten the retaining screw *(above)*.

13 **Connecting the water supply.** Use a T compression fitting to lead a length of pipe from the vertical supply pipe. Bring this extension behind the W.C. and then upwards, using an elbow compression fitting for the bend to meet the threaded water inlet pipe at the base of the cistern. Join the two pipes with a tap connector.

14 **Fitting the overflow pipe.** Attach a plastic overflow pipe to the base of the cistern, using a compression fitting and two plastic elbow joints as shown above. Drill a hole through the outside wall using a power drill and masonry bit. Make sure that the pipe slopes slightly downwards and extends at least 100 mm beyond the outside wall. Make good the hole. Turn on the water supply.

Installing a Washing Machine

Plumbing in an automatic washing machine entails tapping existing supplies to conduct hot and cold water to the machine, and installing a waste with an open standpipe to receive the machine's outlet hose and lead the dirty water away. This is a straightforward job, especially if—as in the project on these pages—the machine is sited against an outside wall beside the kitchen sink; the sink's supplies can then conveniently be tapped, and the machine's waste taken through the wall to run parallel with that of the sink and discharge into the outside drain.

The precise route taken by the waste pipe will depend on individual circumstances. Once you have led it through the external wall it may, for instance, be possible to unite it to the sink's waste, using push-fit connectors and ensuring that there is a downward gradient from the new waste to the existing one.

If the sink is alongside an internal wall it will have a waste extension to the nearest external wall. The washing machine waste can be joined to this by means of a T-fitting and a new length of pipe.

An alternative is to dispense with a separate washing machine waste and run the outlet hose directly into the sink's own waste system. To do this, the sink's trap is replaced with a special fitting that will accommodate the outlet hose (see page 38 for changing a sink trap).

When deciding where to site your washing machine, bear in mind that floor-standing machines are all designed to a standard height. Front-loaders can be slipped under a draining-board or work surface. Top-loaders are sometimes fitted with a laminate top to serve as a work surface when the machine is not in use.

For the supply extensions described in this project you will need 15 mm copper piping, two T-fittings, two elbow fittings and two shut-off valves compatible with the washing machine's supply hoses. For the waste installation, you will need a standard washing machine waste assembly unit, two lengths of 40 mm plastic waste pipe, plastic brackets, a plastic swept T-fitting with a screw-on rodding eye, a plastic elbow fitting, solvent cement to seal the connections, and cleaning fluid (best obtained at the same time as the solvent and fittings to ensure compatability).

1 Tapping the sink supplies. Turn off the mains stop-tap and drain the rising main by turning on the sink's cold tap. Isolate the hot supply by turning off the valve on the cold feed pipe supplying the hot water cylinder, and then draining the sink's hot tap. Measure and cut two lengths of 15 mm copper pipe to extend the sink supplies horizontally, replacing the existing elbows with T compression fittings. Run the machine's cold supply to a point about 70 mm from the edge of the sink unit, and the hot supply to a point about 70 mm to the left.

With elbow fittings and two further lengths of piping, run the supplies upwards to a point near the top of the machine. To the ends of the supplies attach safety shut-off valves *(inset, below)*, which should be kept closed when the washing machine is not in use.

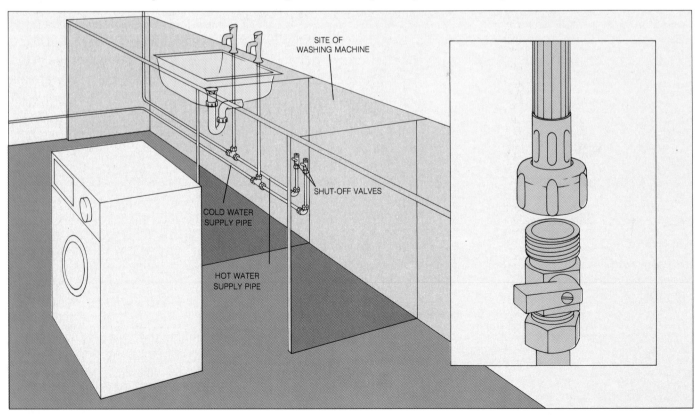

SITE OF WASHING MACHINE

SHUT-OFF VALVES

COLD WATER SUPPLY PIPE

HOT WATER SUPPLY PIPE

2 **Drilling an outlet for the waste.** Having marked the external wall at an appropriate spot, drill a series of holes to make an opening through the wall slightly larger than 40 mm in diameter *(below)*. Alternatively make the hole with a hammer and cold chisel. The new outlet should be sited according to the manufacturer's recommendations; in this project it is to the right of the extended water supplies and close to the side of a kitchen unit to the right of the washing machine site.

3 **Assembling the plastic waste.** A standard washing machine waste fitting incorporates a swivel P-trap, the short end of which is equipped with a compression nut which connects to the 40 mm outlet pipe. Connect the trap to the outlet pipe by tightening the nut *(below)*. The long end of the trap serves as a standpipe, its diameter sufficient for the machine's outlet hose to fit loosely inside it, with an air-gap all round.

4 **Positioning the waste.** Holding the trap firmly, push the outlet pipe through the hole in the wall *(below)*. The waste unit is in position when the compression nut almost touches the wall; there should be enough room to unscrew it later if necessary. Once the exterior work on the waste has been completed, the standpipe will be secured to the unit wall with brackets.

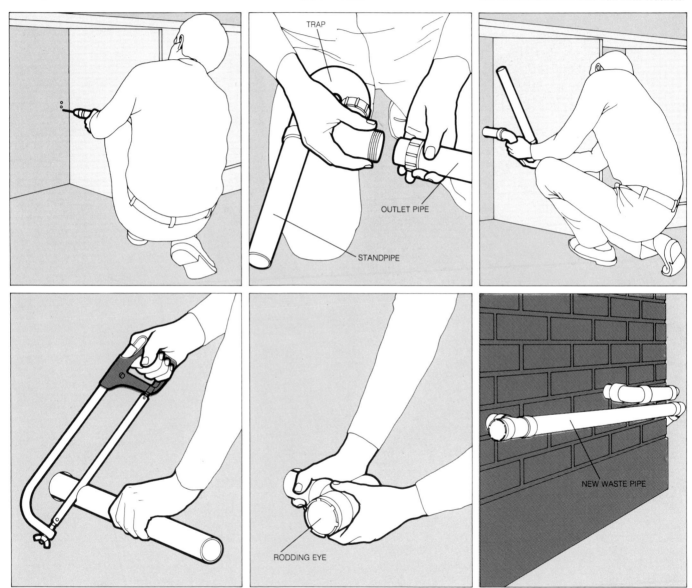

5 **Trimming the outlet pipe.** Trim the outlet pipe outside the house so that only about 40 mm sticks through the wall. To cut the pipe, hold it firmly in position with one hand and saw through it squarely with a hacksaw *(above)*. Smooth the cut edges with the reaming edge of a pipe cutter, or else with a fine file.

6 **Measuring up the external waste.** Make a dry assembly of the external waste by attaching the T-fitting to the end of the outlet pipe and screwing the rodding eye on to the end of the T that is pointing away from the drain

(above, left). Cut a length of plastic pipe to reach the corner of the house *(above)*. Attach an elbow fitting; cut a second length of plastic pipe to run from the elbow diagonally downwards to reach the outside gulley.

7 **Completing the external waste.** Dismantle the dry assembly and slip a bracket over the waste pipe. Use cleaning fluid to prepare all the surfaces to be joined. Applying solvent cement, reassemble the external waste, section by section starting at the T-fitting. Screw the bracket to the wall near the elbow at the corner.

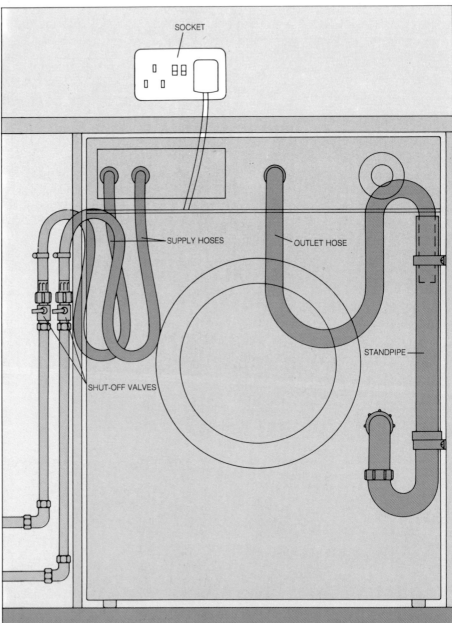

SOCKET

SUPPLY HOSES

OUTLET HOSE

STANDPIPE

SHUT-OFF VALVES

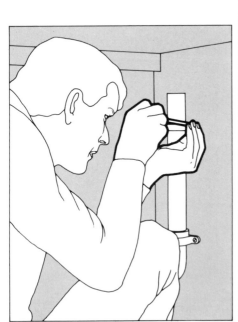

8 **Securing the internal waste.** Making use of the trap's swivel mechanism, manoeuvre the standpipe into the correct position against the unit wall. Secure it in place with two plastic brackets (*above*).

9 **The completed installation.** Move the washing machine into a position where you can connect it to the supplies. Fit the machine's rubber supply hoses on to the ends of the safety shut-off valves, ensuring that the hot and cold hoses correspond to the appropriate supply pipes. Insert the end of the outlet hose into the standpipe. Push the machine into place against the wall as far as the pipes will allow. Turn on the water supplies.

If there is no socket nearby to connect the machine to the electricity supply, install a new one rather than extend the machine's electric cord hazardously across the kitchen floor.

Fitting an Outside Tap

Many outdoor tasks, such as watering the garden or washing the car, are accomplished more efficiently with the aid of an outside tap. You can easily install one yourself, using a length of 15 mm copper pipe to extend a branch of the rising main through an outside wall, and then fitting a hose-union bib tap. For this project you may require permission from your local water authority, who may impose an additional water rate.

When choosing a site for a tap, bear in mind the distance the connecting pipe will have to run; it is usually easiest to tee it from that branch of the rising main serving the cold tap of the kitchen sink. Make sure that the tap will be at a convenient height for either filling a watering can or attaching a hose.

Besides copper piping you will need one T compression fitting and two elbow compression fittings, as well as a backplate elbow fitting with which to secure the tap to exterior wall. Also necessary is a stoptap to be fitted inside the house so that in winter you can turn off the water if there is any danger of the exterior pipe freezing.

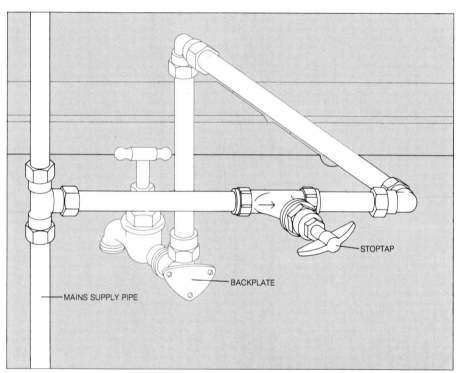

MAINS SUPPLY PIPE

BACKPLATE

STOPTAP

1 **Leading the supply outside.** With the mains supply turned off and the rising main drained, fit a 15 mm compression T-fitting to the rising main *(page 53)*. To the T-fitting attach a short section of 15 mm copper pipe and a stoptap, with its arrow pointing away from the mains. Extend the supply with a further length of piping and add an elbow compression fitting so that it is aligned with the point where the pipe will pass through the wall.

Use a power drill fitted with a masonry bit to make a hole through the wall slightly larger than 15 mm in diameter. Measure and cut a length of pipe to go from the elbow through the wall and extend beyond it for about 20 mm. Fit this pipe, and to its open end attach a second elbow pointing downwards. Attach another section of pipe, its length dictated by the required height of the tap above the ground.

Hold the backplate elbow in position on the downpipe and mark through the screw holes on to the wall. Remove the backplate, drill the holes and insert wall plugs. Replace the backplate and screw it in position. Tighten the compression nut with a pipe wrench. Use a mastic cement, or sand and cement, to make good the brickwork round the hole.

2 **Attaching the tap.** After applying jointing compound or PTFE tape to the thread of the bib tap, fit the tap into the threaded socket of the backplate elbow and screw it into place. Open the internal stoptap and test the installation.

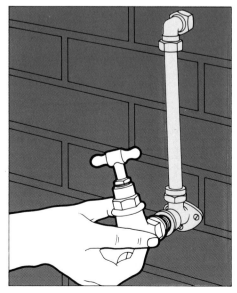

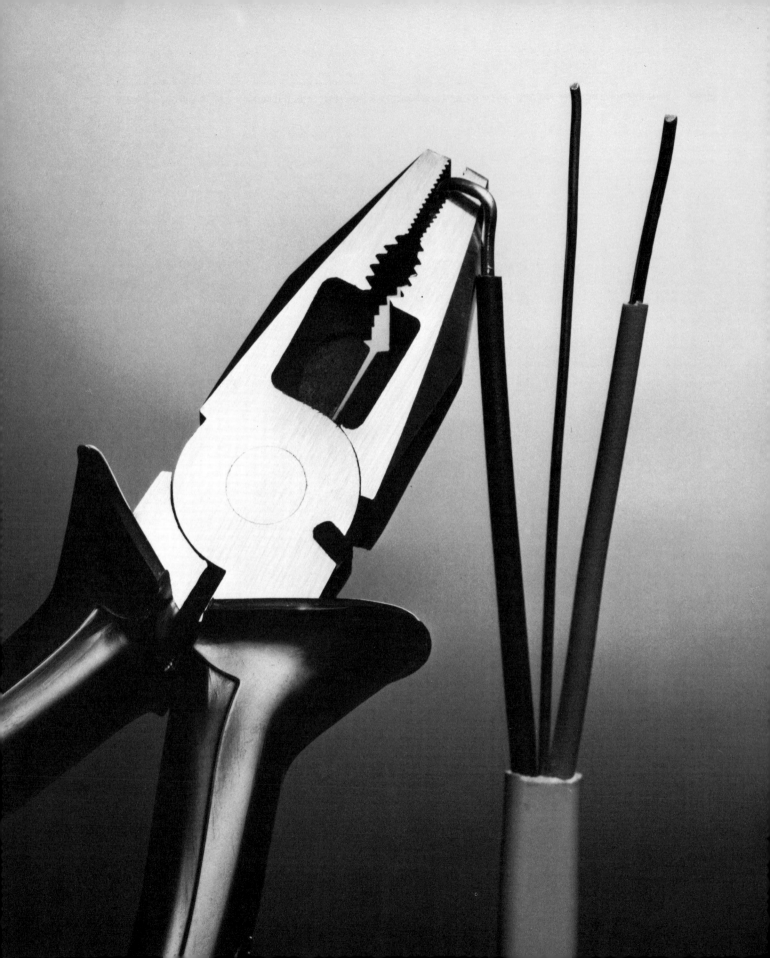

5 A Guide for the Home Electrician

Preparing an installation. Long-nose pliers bend a conductor wire for attachment to a screw terminal in the most common operation in electrical work. The PVC-sheathed cable, which contains two sheathed and one bare copper wire, is the kind used in most house wiring.

Working with wiring is something that many house owners are unwilling to do for themselves. Electricity appears to be mysterious, even baffling; electrical jobs seem to hold an aura of danger. Like many other misconceptions, these beliefs are built up from small grains of truth—or even from no truth at all.

Take the idea that electrical jobs are complex and laborious. In fact, they are straightforward and, in the great majority of cases, surprisingly easy. Procedures and equipment are standardized. The techniques of wiring actually call for less manual skill than most other home repair jobs. When you are replacing a defective switch in a wall, for instance, the job involves a few turns of a screwdriver, a stop at an electrical goods shop and about 10 minutes' work—all at a cost of a pound or two.

Some home owners have a vague feeling that working on their own wiring is illegal. In fact, there are no laws in Britain to restrict do-it-yourself wiring. However, you should ensure that all electrical work in the home complies with the Regulations for Electrical Installations which are published by, and obtainable from, the Institution of Electrical Engineers (I.E.E.) at Hitchin, Hertfordshire. These regulations are concerned mainly with safety and, although they are not legally enforceable, your local electricity board could refuse to connect up an installation which failed to meet the specified standards.

Another deterrent is the fear that doing your own wiring will automatically compromise your fire insurance cover. In fact, this fear is unfounded; the typical house insurance policy has no provision covering do-it-yourself electrical work. However, if a fire was caused by wiring you had installed, the insurance company might decide that you were a poor risk and be reluctant to renew your policy.

Indeed, fear of causing a fire, combined with concern over the possibility of suffering an electric shock, is probably the greatest deterrent to tackling your own wiring. Here the grain of truth in the common belief is real, for electricity can certainly be dangerous—even lethal. But the danger can be avoided by observing the basic safety rules and procedures that are listed on page 100.

Although you can work on your own home wiring without any knowledge of electrical theory, you should acquaint yourself with some electrical terms and concepts. To explain an electrical supply system, an analogy—only an analogy, and not entirely accurate—is often made with a water supply system. The generator of a power station is likened to the pumps of a reservoir, the service cables to the water supply mains, and the wires of house circuits to domestic water pipes. In the water system, pressure that is created by the pumps pushes water through the supply mains and into home piping. In the same way, voltage that is created by the generator pushes electric current through the service cables and into the wires of house circuits.

Inside a house, the current flows through "live" wires (technically referred to as "phase"), comparable to the pressurized supply pipes of a plumbing system. At various points along these wires are outlets in the form of switches, sockets and ceiling roses. Turning on a light switch is rather like turning on a tap to let water run—an electrical current flows through the live wires to make the wire filament of the bulb glow.

Once the current has done its work, its voltage drops to zero, just as water loses pressure after flowing through a sink or wash basin. And the electrical system has "drains"—the black neutral wires that return the current to its source—just as a plumbing system has drain pipes through which water runs into the sewer mains or the ground. In addition, the electrical system has an extra set of drains, called earth wires *(page 96)*, which provide a safety mechanism in the event of some fault developing in a circuit or an appliance.

In a plumbing system, the rate of the water flow is determined partly by pressure and partly by the size of the pipe. Thus, a very narrow pipe allows less water to flow than a wide pipe. Similarly, the rate at which current flows through a wire is determined partly by voltage and partly by the size of the wire. In general, the thicker the conductor wire, the less the resistance—and the less the resistance, the greater the flow of current. (Electricians measure this resistance in ohms and the flow of current in amperes, or amps.)

Here, however, the analogy breaks down. For, unlike water flowing through a pipe, electric current flowing through a wire generates heat—heat which increases in proportion to the amount of resistance the current encounters. It is essential, therefore, in installing a circuit, to ensure that the wires are large enough to conduct current at the required rate *(page 95)*. Otherwise they will become overheated and may even cause a fire. In practice, most domestic wiring is carried out using two basic sizes—1 mm^2 for lighting circuits and 2.5 mm^2 for socket outlet circuits. It is usually only when a heavy current is required—as with electric cookers or shower heaters, for example— that the basic size of the wiring needs to be increased.

As well as being the right size, the wires, or conductors, must also be made of the right materials. Most metals conduct electricity, but some are better conductors than others, offering less resistance to the flow of current and so causing the current to generate less heat. Copper, which is particularly good, is the conductor most commonly used; brass—a copper alloy—is used where copper would be too soft; and aluminium is used where copper would be too heavy or expensive. On the other hand, it is through resistance that electricity is harnessed to provide heat, light and power. Thus, the fittings and appliances which run off a circuit, unlike the circuit itself, are designed with resistive materials— for example, the tungsten filaments of an incandescent lamp or the heating element of an electric fire.

At the opposite end of the scale to conductors are insulators. These do not normally allow current to flow and are used to encase live parts, such as wires, sockets and plugs. Most non-metals are insulators, but plastic, porcelain and rubber are the materials usually found in electrical systems. Air is also a good insulator; that is to say, it is such a poor conductor that the overhead wires conveying electricity around the country need only be insulated when they are in contact with pylons or poles—or when they come down to the ground.

Indeed, the earth is such a good conductor that electricity will take any opportunity to flow into it. This is why you are liable to get a shock if you touch a live wire while standing on the ground. It is also why every circuit must have an earth wire running in parallel with the live and neutral wires. Thus, if the live wire comes into accidental contact with a conductive material—for example, the metal casing of an electric kettle or toaster—the current is diverted, or short-circuited, directly to earth. At the same time, the low resistance of the earth causes a much larger current to flow, and this, in turn, usually activates the essential safety device—the fuse *(pages 93–94)*.

A fuse consists of a length of thin wire and is designed to be the weak link in a circuit. If, as a result of an overload or a fault, too much current is passed through, the fuse will melt or "blow", thereby breaking the circuit before the build-up of heat reaches a dangerous level. An alternative to the fuse is the M.C.B. (miniature circuit breaker). Used in the more modern types of installation, the M.C.B. cuts off the supply automatically when excess current flows through the circuit. The switch or button is simply reset by hand when the overload has been removed or the fault has been corrected.

The other components of an electrical system are equally easy to understand. The conductors—cable for fixed wiring and "flex" (flexible cord) for connecting the fixed wiring to appliances and light fittings— are nowadays mostly insulated and sheathed with PVC. The electrical "hardware"—plugs, sockets, ceiling roses, switches and lampholders— are usually made of moulded plastic, though some accessories may have metal casings. The terminals for connecting wires within the fittings are labelled E or ⊕ for earth, L or P for live or phase, and N for neutral. In addition, the wires are colour coded, so that you can match them with the appropriate terminals. Thus, in cable, the red wire goes to live, the black to neutral and the bare conductor is sheathed in green and yellow and goes to earth; in flex, the green and yellow wire goes to earth, the brown to live and the blue to neutral.

Working on any of these components requires no more expertise than changing a light bulb. However, you should always follow two cardinal safety rules. Never embark on an electrical job if you have the slightest doubt that it is within your capabilities. And never work on a cable or fixed appliance unless the relevant circuit is dead. This means that it should not simply be switched off, but also isolated from the supply—either by the removal of the fuse or by the switching off of the supply itself at the mains position.

Making and Using a Continuity Tester

Consisting mainly of a battery, a bulb and two leads, a continuity tester shows if an electrical component—a switch or lamp socket, for instance—is working correctly. Having disconnected the component from the mains, you simply attach it to the leads of the tester. If the bulb lights, there is a continuous path for the current. If the bulb does not light, there is a break in the path—and you need a new component.

A continuity tester is easily made. Buy a 6 volt bulb and a lampholder, and connect a piece of thin flex to each of the lampholder terminals. Using a thick rubber band, secure the lampholder to a 4.5 volt battery with flat-type terminals. Join the flex from the positive terminal of the lampholder to the positive terminal of the battery. Connect the free end of the other flex to a crocodile clip. Run a third piece of flex from the negative battery terminal to a second crocodile clip, and attach both clips to the component you wish to test.

Testing a cartridge fuse. There is usually no external evidence of damage when a cartridge fuse blows *(page 94)*, so if an appliance fails to operate, the only way of determining whether the fault lies with the fuse is by using a continuity tester. Remove the fuse and clamp the crocodile clips of the test leads to the metal end caps. If the bulb lights, the fuse is good; the trouble lies elsewhere. If the bulb does not light, the fuse is blown; replace it with a new one.

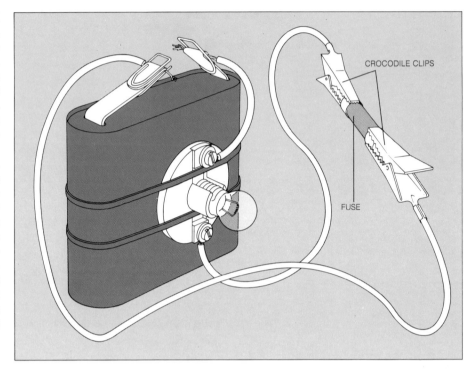

CROCODILE CLIPS

FUSE

Volts, Amps, Ohms and Watts

When working on your house wiring or buying electrical equipment, you will constantly come across references to the following units of measure. Each unit has a specific significance, and the first four bear a relationship to one another.
□ VOLT (often expressed simply as V) is a measure of the pressure that pushes the current round a circuit. The current supplied to domestic premises in the U.K. is generally at a pressure of 240V, though it may vary about 14V above or below that figure.

As the current moves from the live wire through the load presented by an appliance or lamp, its conversion to energy causes the voltage to drop. When the current leaves the load and returns through the neutral wire to its source at the power station, the voltage is down to almost zero.
□ AMPERE (amp, or A, for short) is the unit used to measure the amount of current—that is, the number of electri-

cally charged particles called electrons—that flows past a given point on a circuit each second. Billions of electrons are necessary to make up 1 ampere. Amperage is determined partly by voltage—and partly by resistance.
□ OHM (symbol Ω) is the unit for measuring resistance. It is named after a 19th-century German physicist, Georg Simon Ohm, who established the law that states that the current flow through a conductor is inversely proportional to the resistance. This may be expressed by the equation: Volts ÷ ohms = amps. Thus, if you know two of the amounts involved, you can work out the third.

The term impedance is sometimes used instead of resistance; there is a technical difference between these terms, but for house wiring the words are interchangeable.
□ WATT (W) is the unit of power, indicating how much current an appliance

consumes at any given moment. The relation between volts, amps and watts is expressed in another equation that enables you to make any calculations you may need for the projects in this book: volts × amps = watts.

Thus, if the current is 240V and an appliance requires 4A of current, the equation will read: 240V × 4A = 960W. Conversely, if you have an appliance rated at 1,200W, you can calculate that the amount of current required is 5A. That is: 1,200W ÷ 240V = 5A.

It is customary to use the kilowatt (kW), which is 1,000 watts, as the unit of power for higher wattages.
□ KILOWATT–HOUR is the unit for measuring the total amount of electricity consumed. For example, if you burned a 1 kW fire for exactly 1 hour, it would draw 1 kilowatt–hour (kWh) of energy from the mains—a unit of consumption that would be included in your next electricity bill.

A Basic Tool Kit for Home Wiring

Tools for the electrical repair and improvement jobs in this book are few in number and require only a modest investment. Some of them may already be in your home tool kit—for example, such general-purpose devices as an electric drill, screwdrivers, saws, a hammer and a chisel. Others are more specialized and may need to be added.

□ TORCH. Always keep a torch by the fuse board or consumer unit *(page 93)*. Then, if a fuse on a light circuit blows during the night, you will not have to grope about in the dark to repair or replace it *(page 94)*.

□ PLIERS. Two kinds are needed for electrical work. Long-nose pliers have elongated jaws that are ideal for bending a loop in the end of light-gauge wire so that it can be attached to a terminal. The jaws should be serrated to provide a firm grip and there should be cutting edges near the pivot so that you can snip the wire. Electrician's pliers are used for bending and shaping heavy-gauge wiring and for twisting out removable parts from certain electrical components. These pliers should also have cutting edges and serrated jaws.

□ DIAGONAL CUTTERS. Although electrician's pliers can be used to cut cable *(page 95)*, a pair of diagonal cutters will make the job much easier.

□ WIRE STRIPPERS. As the name suggests wire strippers remove the insulation from electrical wiring *(page 101)*. In the type shown below, there is a notched cutting edge at the end of each arm and a screw for adjusting the arms to the thickness of the wire. The cutting edges sever the insulation enclosing the wire but stop short of the wire itself, allowing the insulation to be pulled away.

□ KNIFE. A sharp knife is needed to slit and then trim back the tough PVC sheathing round cable. A utility knife with a retractable blade is suitable.

□ TERMINAL SCREWDRIVER. You need a variety of screwdrivers for wiring jobs, but the one you will use most frequently is the terminal type with parallel-sided tip.

Although each of the tools shown below is properly insulated, views differ about the value of insulation. On the one hand, it is regarded as unnecessary since work should never be carried out on live circuits *(page 100)*. On the other hand, insulation is regarded as a wise safety precaution in the event of mistakes.

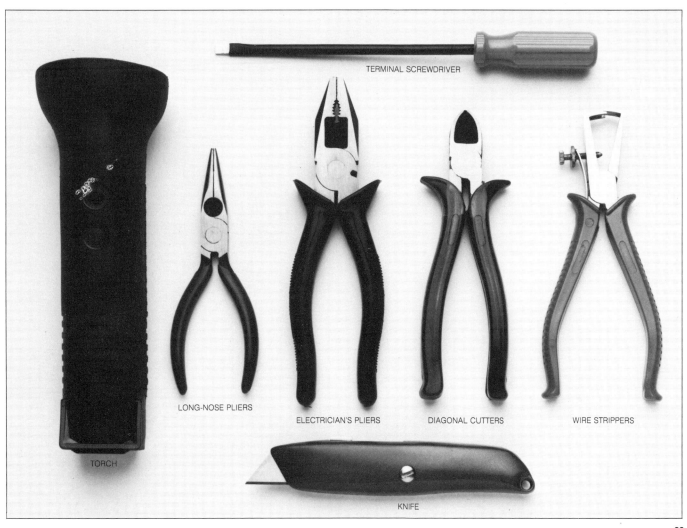

TERMINAL SCREWDRIVER

LONG-NOSE PLIERS

ELECTRICIAN'S PLIERS

DIAGONAL CUTTERS

WIRE STRIPPERS

TORCH

KNIFE

The Multiple Pathways of Electric Current

Electricity generated in the power station comes into your home at 240 volts and is transmitted by a service cable which terminates in a sealed unit containing the Electricity Board's service fuse. This is generally rated at 100 amps, but 60 or 80 amps is possible in older houses. This fuse provides a last defence in the unlikely event that your own fuses or M.C.B.s (miniature circuit breakers) fail to operate.

From the sealed fuse unit, the current passes through a meter *(overleaf)*, which records the amount used, and flows on through a consumer unit *(page 93)*. This incorporates the fuses or M.C.B.s for all the house circuits. The cables of these circuits convey the current from the consumer unit (or, in older installations, the fuse board) to lights, switches and socket outlets.

Each circuit has a specific current rating determined by the maximum load it is expected to carry *(page 99)*. There are four standard current ratings—5 amps for lighting, and 15, 20 and 30 amps for power. A fifth rating—45 amps—has recently been introduced for "electricaire" central heating units and large electric cookers.

Each of the two principal types of circuit—lighting and power—may be based on one or other of two wiring systems.

□ RING FINAL CIRCUIT WIRING. In houses wired since 1947, most or all of the power is supplied by a ring final circuit—so called because the circuit is wired in the form of a continuous ring starting and ending at a single 30 amp fuse or M.C.B. in the consumer unit. A ring final circuit can supply any number of 13 amp socket outlets and fixed appliances, provided only that the total floor area covered by the circuit does not exceed 100 square metres.

In addition, branch cables called spurs may be run from the ring cable to supply socket outlets in remote positions—for example, a loft or basement. The number of spurs must not exceed the number of socket outlets and fixed appliances connected directly to the ring, and each spur may only supply one single or one double outlet. A spur is connected to the ring cable at the terminals of a ring socket outlet or at a 30 amp joint box inserted into the ring.

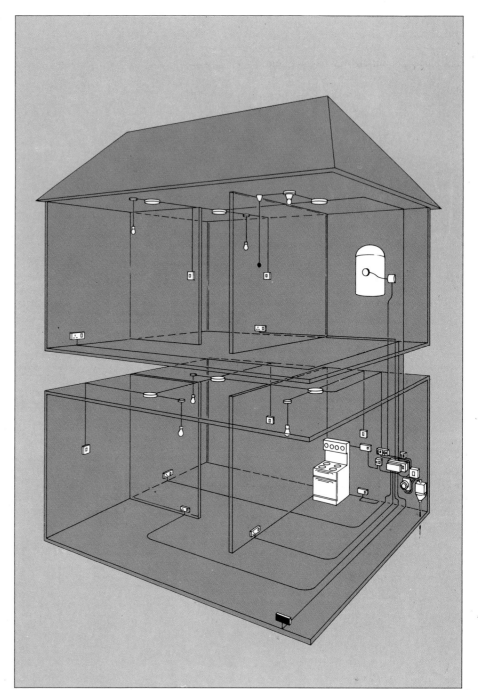

Old wiring. In a house with pre-1947 radial wiring, the circuits run from a number of separate fuse boxes, each with its own mains switch. All the power circuits are connected to one socket outlet or one fixed appliance apiece, and the socket outlets are designed to take round-pin plugs of 2, 5 or 15 amps. The lighting circuits—usually one for each floor—run to joint boxes fixed between the ceiling joists. From each joint box one cable goes to the corresponding light switch and another goes to the ceiling rose.

□ RADIAL WIRING. As with a ring final circuit, the function of a radial power circuit is to supply power for a number of 13 amp socket outlets and fixed appliances. However, whereas a ring final circuit terminates back at the consumer unit, a radial circuit terminates at the last outlet.

Furthermore, the maximum floor area that may be covered by a radial circuit is much less than that for a ring final circuit. A radial circuit of 20 amp current rating may supply an unlimited number of outlets and appliances within an area of 20 square metres, and one of 30 amp rating may supply an unlimited number within an area of 50 square metres.

Generally, radial circuits are best used to supplement ring final circuits, particularly in a kitchen with a large range of electrical appliances. However, an appliance with a load in excess of 3,000 watts (3kW) should be wired on its own individual circuit protected at the consumer unit by a 30 or 45 amp fuse or M.C.B.

In fact, all power circuits installed before 1947 were wired to just one socket outlet or fixed appliance apiece. The outlets were designed to take round-pin plugs of 2, 5 or 15 amps—the then standard current ratings—and the plugs did not contain their own fuses. If you have round-pin outlets and the circuits run from a number of separate fuse boxes, each with its own mains switch, then you can be fairly certain that the wiring is more than 35 years old.

In that case, you should have the wiring checked as soon as possible, since it will certainly have deteriorated and may even be dangerous. Indeed, the electricity boards have declared that "any house over 25 years old may have dangerous wiring".

□ JOINT-BOX WIRING. In many houses built before 1966, the lighting circuit runs from a 5 amp fuse in the consumer unit to a series of joint boxes fixed between ceiling joists. From each box run two more cables—one to the corresponding switch, the other to the ceiling rose *(page 107)*.

□ LOOP-IN WIRING. A modern lighting installation is most likely to use the loop-in system—so called because the supply cable runs direct from one ceiling rose to another until all the roses are linked, or looped in, together. One cable is run from each ceiling rose to its corresponding switch. The maximum number of lights recommended for any circuit, whether of the joint box or loop-in variety, is eight.

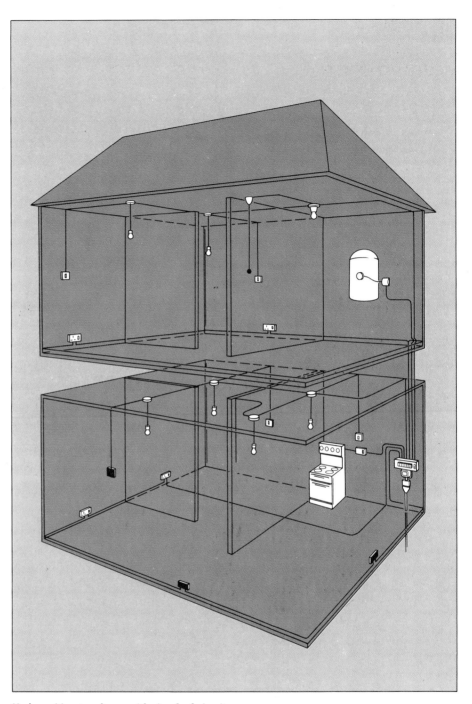

Modern wiring. In a house with ring final circuit wiring, all the circuits run from a consumer unit with a single mains switch. Socket outlets are designed to take square-pin plugs of 13 amps and are connected by a continuous ring of cable. In most cases, one ring serves the upstairs socket outlets, and a second supplies those on the ground floor. In the same way, each floor is usually served by its own lighting circuit running direct from one ceiling rose to another. A cable goes from each ceiling rose to its corresponding switch. There are separate circuits for large fixed appliances.

The Meter

Your meter includes a small disc which revolves a certain number of times for every kWh (kilowatt–hour) or unit of electricity consumed. The disc operates, in turn, numbered indicators to register the amount of current used.

Some meters have digital dials that resemble the milometer of a car, and they are read in the same way. More common, however, is the clock-type meter *(right)* with five separate dials, each of which supplies one digit for the reading. The lower dial, which is red, shows fractions of a unit and is used only for test purposes.

The left-hand dial registers tens of thousands, the next thousands, and so on to the right-hand dial, which registers single units. The numbers on the dials are arranged alternately clockwise and anticlockwise, and the pointers on the dials move accordingly.

When taking a reading, start with the left-hand dial and work across to the right of the meter. If a pointer is between two numbers, always take the lower number. If a pointer is directly over a number, the clue to a correct reading is provided by looking at the adjoining dial, as explained in the example on the right.

To check your electricity bills, as you should periodically, make two consecutive readings and subtract the first from the second to calculate the consumption for the intervening period. Take each reading on the day the official from the Electricity Board calls to make his own reading. Then compare your results with the figures on the second bill.

How can you check if your meter is working accurately? The simplest way is by making use of the red dial, which measures 0.1 (or 1/10) of a unit. First, switch off all electrical equipment in the house and make sure that the rotating disc is stationary.

Note the position of the pointer on the red dial and then switch on a load of 1 kW—for instance, of a 1 kW electric fire. If the meter is working accurately, the pointer should make one revolution—equivalent to one whole unit—in an hour.

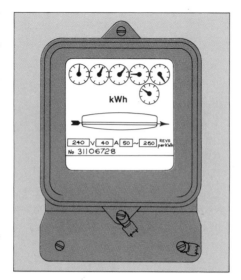

Reading a clock-type meter. The meter shown here *(left)* has a reading of 99,124 kWh and will help you to understand the procedure involved. Start with the left-hand dial, making sure to note in each case which way the pointer rotates *(below)*. If the pointer is between two numbers, always take the lower number.

If the pointer is directly over a number, look at the pointer on the next dial to the right—if it is between 0 and 1, then the correct number to write down for the dial you are reading is the number actually indicated. But if the dial to the right registers between 9 and 0, then you should write down one digit less than the number indicated. For example, the pointer on the first dial is at 0, but as the pointer on the second dial is between 9 and 0, the number to note is 9. The reason is simple: the pointer of the right-hand dial must make one complete revolution before the dial to its left moves ahead one digit.

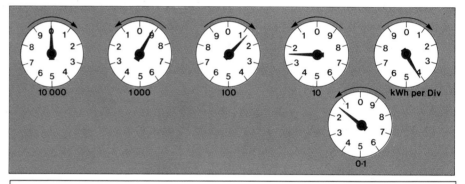

Cutting Down on Electricity Bills

You can trim ever-increasing electricity bills by installing various energy-saving devices. For example:
☐ Fluorescent lights *(page 108)*, which provide more light than incandescent bulbs of the same wattage, consume less energy for an equivalent light output and last much longer.
☐ Dimmer switches, which reduce power consumption by allowing decreased lighting levels that suit varying needs.
☐ Switches with pilot lights that warn when an out-of-the-way light or appliance has been forgotten.

Other ways of reducing electricity costs do not require special equipment but simply involve changes in habits of buying or using lights and appliances.
☐ Use a single bulb of higher wattage rather than several low-watt bulbs. Two 60 watt bulbs produce less light than one 100 watt bulb, though they consume about 20 per cent more energy and cost more to buy.

☐ Use long-life bulbs only when their longevity outweighs the fact that they emit only 80 per cent of the light of standard bulbs of the same wattage.
☐ Buy lampshades that are wide at both ends—they spread light better than shades wih narrow openings.
☐ If you have an immersion heater, check that the cylinder is properly insulated. This will slow down the loss of heat out of the cylinder so that less energy will be needed to maintain the water at the correct temperature.
☐ Before you buy a large appliance check the amount of energy it consumes. This information usually appears on an appliance's data plate, expressed in watts. Compare this wattage with that of appliances made by other manufacturers. If all other factors are equal, choose the appliance with the lowest wattage rating.
☐ Study the cheap-rate tariffs offered by your Electricity Board and see whether they can be used to advantage.

Fuses and Circuit Breakers

From the electricity meter, the current passes to a consumer unit with an integral mains switch, or, in older installations, to a fuse board with separate switches and fuse boxes. The power is then transferred to the wiring circuits either by means of individual fuses *(below, left)* or by circuit breakers *(below, right)*.

Either type of device serves an essential safety function. If a fault or an overload results in more current flowing through a circuit than it is designed to carry, the fuse will melt or the circuit breaker will open, thereby cutting off the circuit from the mains supply. In this way, the excess current is prevented from generating the kind of heat that usually causes a fire.

Miniature circuit breakers (M.C.B.s) are more convenient than fuses, which have to be repaired or replaced after a circuit interruption. Once the cause of the interruption has been corrected, a circuit breaker is simply reset by pushing the switch or button to the "on" position.

M.C.B.s are a fairly recent development, however, and most electrical installations are still protected by fuses. These are of two types—rewirable and cartridge—and they are housed in porcelain or plastic fuse holders which plug into the fuseways of the consumer unit or fuse box. Plastic holders are usually colour coded according to their current rating: 5 amp is coloured white, 15 amp blue, 20 amp yellow, 30 amp red and 45 amp green.

The most widely used of the two fuses is the rewirable type, in which the fuse element—a piece of thin wire—is held in position by a screw terminal on either side of the holder. If a fuse blows, melting the wire between the terminals, first the remnants of the old wire are removed and then a new piece of the same current rating is fitted in its place *(overleaf)*.

In the case of the cartridge fuse, the element is enclosed in a small, metal-capped tube which slots into two spring contacts on the holder. The disadvantage of a cartridge fuse is that it cannot be repaired; once it has blown, it has to be replaced *(overleaf)*. It is also more expensive to replace than the rewirable type.

On the other hand, cartridge fuses come in different sizes according to their current rating, so that it is impossible to fit, say, a 20 amp fuse into a 5 amp holder. Like plastic fuse holders, cartridge fuses are colour coded so that they can be easily identified. The most important advantage of all is that a cartridge fuse provides greater protection for the circuit than a rewirable fuse. This is because it takes less excess current to blow the cartridge fuse. For example, it would need only 45 amps to blow a 30 amp cartridge fuse compared to about 60 amps for a 30 amp rewirable fuse.

In addition to protecting the circuits in your home, fuses and M.C.B.s perform another and all-important safety function. Because fuses can be removed and M.C.B.s switched off, they enable you to "kill" a circuit so that you can work on it without the risk of receiving a shock.

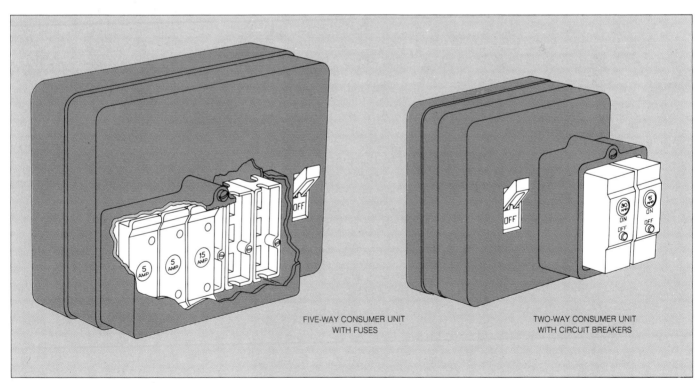

FIVE-WAY CONSUMER UNIT
WITH FUSES

TWO-WAY CONSUMER UNIT
WITH CIRCUIT BREAKERS

Consumer units. Designed for either fuses or M.C.B.s, consumer units are available in a wide range of sizes, from two-way (two fuseways) to 10-way (10 fuseways), which is the largest likely to be required for domestic use. The size is determined by the number of circuits. Thus, a house supplied with five circuits needs a five-way consumer unit *(above, left)*. Often, several spare fuseways are also included so that extra circuits can be added later. The alternative is to run the extra circuits from an additional consumer unit. Where you wish to add one or two new circuits, for example, you must install an extra two-way consumer unit *(above, right)*.

Dealing with Blown Circuit Fuses

If a fuse blows or an M.C.B. trips, cutting off the lights or power in part of the house, turn off the mains switch at the consumer unit and trace the device concerned. This is easy if you have M.C.B.s: the switch will simply have flipped into the "off" position and can be restored to the "on" position as soon as the fault has been rectified.

In the case of fuses, there should be a list on or near the consumer unit showing which device controls which circuit *(page 98)*. If there is no list, then you will need to remove and examine in turn each fuse with the same rating as that of the affected circuit. For example, if a lighting circuit cuts out, then you should check the 5 amp fuses. Where a power circuit cuts out, check the 30 amp fuses—20 amp if you have radial wiring.

Individual appliances such as electric cookers, immersion heaters and night storage heaters will have separate circuits, each with a fuse at the consumer unit. Bear in mind that a cartridge fuse, unlike a rewirable fuse, usually shows no visible signs of damage: it must be checked with a continuity tester *(page 88)*.

Before repairing or replacing a fuse *(right)*, you should try to find out why it blew. Usually, the cause will be obvious. If a fuse blows immediately you switch on a light, then there is probably something wrong with either the bulb or the flex. If a fuse blows after you switch on the light, this could be a sign that the fuse wire has deteriorated with age and is no longer capable of carrying its rated current. However, if the fuse is of the cartridge type, which does not deteriorate, there is probably a fault in the wiring.

A ring final circuit fuse will blow only through serious overloading or, again, because of a fault in the wiring. If there is a fault in an appliance, this will usually blow the plug fuse *(page 102)*, leaving the circuit intact. Where you suspect that the wiring is defective, call in an electrician. Never try to solve a wiring or an overload problem by uprating the fuse: the circuit could become dangerously overheated.

Rewiring a Fuse

Replacing the element. Having removed the fuse holder from the consumer unit, loosen the screw terminals and discard the old fuse wire. Replacement fuse wire is available in three ratings—5, 15 and 30 amps—and is sold ready for use, mounted on a card. Select wire of the correct rating and thread the end into the holder *(right)*. Connect the end to the adjoining terminal. Cut the wire to length and connect the free end to the second terminal. Cut off the surplus wire and plug the holder back into the consumer unit.

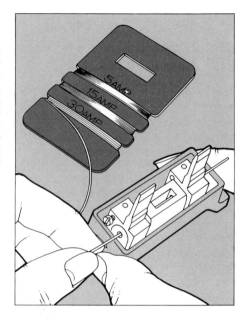

Replacing a Cartridge Fuse

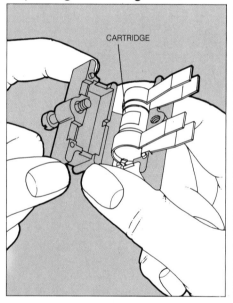

CARTRIDGE

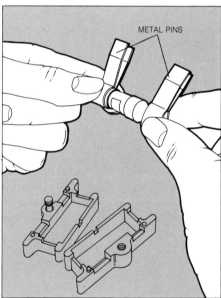

METAL PINS

1 Removing the old cartridge. Unplug the fuse holder from the consumer unit and loosen the retaining screw sufficiently to separate the two parts of the holder *(above)*. The cartridge is secured by two metal pins. Remove these, together with the cartridge itself.

2 Fitting the new cartridge. Pull the pins from the ends of the blown cartridge and fit a new cartridge of the same rating *(above)*. Reinsert the pins into the fuse holder and screw the two parts together again. Plug the fuse holder back into its circuit at the consumer unit.

Varieties of Cable and Flex

Wiring falls into two categories—cable and flex. Cable carries current from the consumer unit to the switches, socket outlets and ceiling roses. Flex provides the link from a socket outlet to an appliance or from a ceiling rose to a lampholder.

The most widely used type of flex consists of two or three PVC-insulated cores, or conductors, encased in protective circular sheathing, also of PVC. The two-core version is connected to pendant light fittings (page 106) and non-earthed appliances. Such appliances are safeguarded by double insulation and carry the symbol of two hollow squares— ▣.

A second type of flex, known as braided circular, is often used for appliances such as electric irons and kettles, which have hot external surfaces. Composed of three synthetic rubber-insulated cores with an overall covering of cotton braid, it can withstand higher temperatures than the normal PVC variety.

Cable is generally made up of two PVC-insulated cores and a bare earth conductor. The exception is the special cable used for two-way switching (page 118), which consists of three insulated cores plus earth. Like flex, cable usually has an outer sheathing of PVC, though for modern wiring this will be flat rather than circular.

The copper conductors of flex are all stranded for greater pliability. Those of cable are stranded or solid depending on their size (right). The size of a conductor is expressed by its cross-sectional area. The larger the conductor, the greater is its current-carrying capacity.

The insulated conductors in three-core flex used to be colour coded red for live, black for neutral and green for earth. In 1971, the colours were changed to brown for live, blue for neutral and green and yellow for earth.

The colour coding for cable with two cores plus earth is the same as for the older type of flex—red (live) and black (neutral). In three-core and earth cable, the insulated conductors are coloured red, yellow and blue. The bare earth conductor must be sleeved with green and yellow insulating material before it is connected to a terminal (page 101).

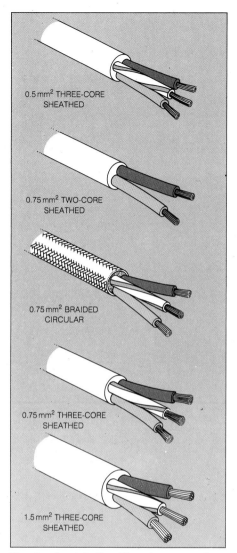

0.5 mm² THREE-CORE SHEATHED

0.75 mm² TWO-CORE SHEATHED

0.75 mm² BRAIDED CIRCULAR

0.75 mm² THREE-CORE SHEATHED

1.5 mm² THREE-CORE SHEATHED

Choosing the right flex. Flex sizes range from 0.5 mm², for low-power appliances such as table lamps and TV sets, to 4 mm², for electric cookers with a power rating up to 6,000 watts. Each size is shown in the table below, together with the appropriate current and power ratings.

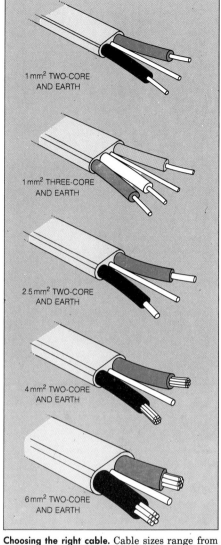

1 mm² TWO-CORE AND EARTH

1 mm² THREE-CORE AND EARTH

2.5 mm² TWO-CORE AND EARTH

4 mm² TWO-CORE AND EARTH

6 mm² TWO-CORE AND EARTH

Choosing the right cable. Cable sizes range from 1 mm², used for lighting circuits, to 16 mm², used for connecting the meter to the consumer unit. Each size is shown below, together with its nominal current rating and application. Usually, only cable larger than 2.5 mm² is stranded.

Flex Sizes and Ratings

Size (mm²)	Current rating (amp)	Power rating of appliance (watts)
0.5	3	720
0.75	6	1,440
1.0	10	2,400
1.5	15	3,600
2.5	20	4,800
4.0	25	6,000

Cable Sizes and Ratings

Size (mm²)	Current rating (amps)	Application
1.0	14	Lighting
1.5	18	Immersion heater or other 15A circuits
2.5	24	Storage heaters, ring final circuits, 15A radial circuits
4.0	32	Small cookers, 30A radial circuits.
6.0	40	Large cookers

Earthing and Bonding for Safety

In a normal electrical circuit, current flows to a light or an appliance through the live wire, and flows back to the power station through the neutral wire, which is connected to the earth. Occasionally, however, something goes wrong with this operation.

If, for example, a piece of flex insulation is damaged, allowing the live wire to make contact with the metal casing of an appliance, then the casing itself becomes live. The danger which then arises is that someone will touch the live metalwork, providing the current with an alternative path to earth—and receiving a possibly lethal shock in the process.

It is for this reason that all electrical appliances—apart from the ones that are double insulated—must be connected to an earth wire *(opposite page)*. In the event of a fault, the earth wire first carries the current along to an earth terminal in the consumer unit. From here, a second wire then takes the current safely to earth—usually via the metal sheathing of the Electricity Board's underground service cable, but sometimes by way of a copper-clad earth rod that is driven into the soil.

Because of its low resistance, the earth wire allows the current to flow at an increased rate, and this, in turn, blows the appropriate fuse or circuit breaker, thereby cutting off the power supply.

Where mains gas and water pipes are made of metal, these should be linked, or bonded, to the electrical earthing system, as shown in the illustration on the opposite page. Other extraneous metalwork, such as sinks, baths and towel rails, should also be bonded to earth. If you are in any doubt about this, then you should consult either the Electricity Board or a qualified electrician as soon as possible.

Tracing a path to earth. The illustration on the right shows the wires and connections that make up a typical earth path. The starting point is the earth terminal attached to the metal base of the toaster. From here, the green and yellow earth wire of the flex runs to the plug and socket outlet, where contact is made with the earth wire of the circuit cable. This wire is connected, in turn, to a main earthing terminal inside the consumer unit. An earthing conductor then runs from this terminal to the means of earthing, which in the illustration is the metal sheathing of the Electricity Board's service cable—the final section of the path back to the power station earth.

The gas and water supply pipes are linked into the earthing system through further lengths of single-core cable, which run from each pipe to the consumer unit.

Earth Leakage Circuit Breakers

If you live in an area where the power is supplied by overhead cables, then your earthing system will probably be connected to an earth electrode—a copper-coated steel rod driven into the ground outside your house.

Used on its own, however, an earth electrode is rarely effective. This is because of its inability to pass large currents into the soil, particularly during dry weather when the resistance of the soil is very high. It must be used, therefore, in conjunction with an earth leakage circuit breaker (E.L.C.B.). This device, which is wired to the consumer unit, automatically cuts off any circuit where an earth leakage occurs.

Of the two types of E.L.C.B.—current operated and voltage operated—it is the current-operated one which is generally recommended. It works on the current-balance principle—that current flowing into a circuit should be equal to current flowing out of it. If there is an imbalance, such as occurs when current leaks into the earthing system, then the E.L.C.B. immediately becomes activated.

Although all E.L.C.B.s operate with great speed and efficiency, not all would provide adequate protection if you touched a live wire while in contact with the ground. Only the high-sensitivity E.L.C.B. *(right)*, which should be fitted as an additional protection to socket-outlet circuits, would give some protection in those circumstances. A current-operated type, it can detect just 30 milliamps of earth current and cut the supply within 30 milliseconds—which is soon enough to help prevent a fatal shock to a person touching a 240 volt live connection.

A disadvantage of the high-sensitivity version is its proneness to "nuisance" tripping due to small earth leakage currents which may not be dangerous. It should be used, therefore, in circuits supplying power tools and other hand-operated appliances where the risk of electric shock is high and occasional nuisance tripping does not matter.

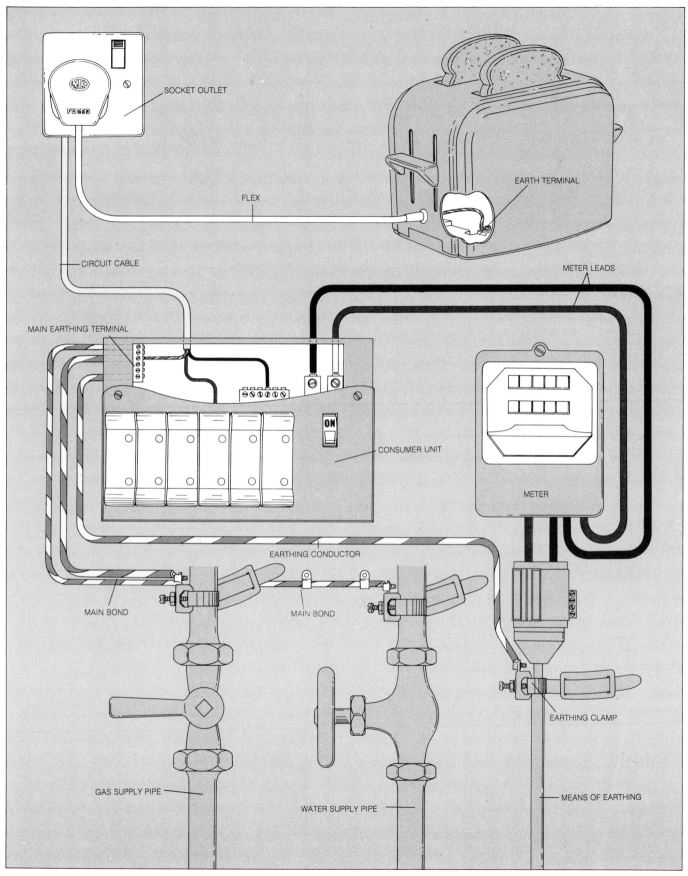

SOCKET OUTLET

EARTH TERMINAL

FLEX

CIRCUIT CABLE

METER LEADS

MAIN EARTHING TERMINAL

ON

CONSUMER UNIT

METER

EARTHING CONDUCTOR

MAIN BOND

MAIN BOND

EARTHING CLAMP

GAS SUPPLY PIPE

WATER SUPPLY PIPE

MEANS OF EARTHING

Mapping an Electrical System

Working on your house wiring is much simpler if you make a map to show which fuse or circuit breaker controls which light, switch and socket outlet. A detailed map enables you to pinpoint trouble, to avoid overloads and to determine which parts of the house will be affected if you disconnect a circuit to work on it.

Before you start mapping, make sure that each fuse or circuit breaker at the consumer unit has a distinguishing number. If they are not numbered, you do it starting from the mains switch. Then prepare your map. Use one sheet for each floor or even each room, indicating the location of all lights, switches and socket outlets.

Next, taking one room at a time, turn on all lights and portable appliances, such as a record player or TV. Do not include fixed appliances, such as an electric cooker or immersion heater—each has an individual circuit, which can be identified later. If a single-socket outlet is not in use, plug a small appliance—either a light or an elec-tric fire—into it. In the case of a double-socket outlet, you need plug into only one of the outlets, since both will be wired on the same circuit.

At the consumer unit, remove each fuse or switch off each circuit breaker in turn. Note the number on your map, together with the lights or appliances that stop working. (An assistant to relay this information saves running back and forth.) Keep the map sections near the consumer unit for easy reference.

A guide to electrical work. In this plan of a first floor in a house, each outlet—switch, light fixture or socket outlet (key, below)—is identified by the number assigned to the fuse or circuit breaker controlling it. Such a sketch indicates which outlets will be affected if you turn off the supply to a circuit, and which fuse or circuit breaker to check when a circuit fails.

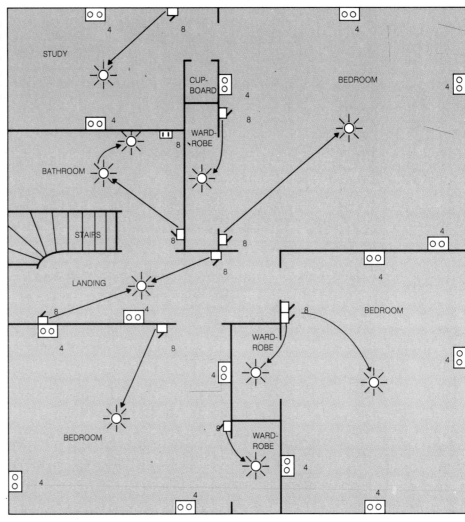

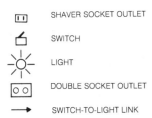

SHAVER SOCKET OUTLET

SWITCH

LIGHT

DOUBLE SOCKET OUTLET

SWITCH-TO-LIGHT LINK

Calculating Electrical Loads

Although a power circuit can supply any number of socket outlets within its prescribed floor area *(page 90)*, the amount of current that can be drawn from it at any one time is limited by the size of the cable. If the current flow becomes too great, then the controlling fuse or circuit breaker is activated, cutting off power to the outlets.

Plugging in an extra table lamp is unlikely to overload a circuit—such devices consume only a small amount of current—but appliances such as toasters and kettles are another matter. You must check before adding a heavy power user that a circuit will be able to cope with the extra load.

List lights and other devices, including any additions, that will operate simultaneously on the circuit, noting the wattage for each one. (This figure is printed on incandescent bulbs and on the data plates of appliances.) Add the wattages together and then divide the total by 240—the mains voltage—to get the amperage. Alternatively, multiply the amperage of the circuit by 240, which will give you its wattage. Either way, the total figure for all the electrical appliances that will be used simultaneously must not exceed the one for the circuit.

The same calculations also apply in respect of lighting circuits. Bear in mind, however, that where a bulb of under 100 watts is fitted, it should be assumed to have a 100 watt rating. This is to ensure against accidental overloading—for example, through the replacement of a blown 60 watt bulb with one of 100 watts.

Where you wish to extend your electrical system—by running a new circuit to a garage, say, or an outside workshop—the first step is to find out the load capacity of the Electricity Board's service cable. This is measured in amps and is sometimes marked on the sealed unit containing the service fuse. If it is not marked, you will have to ask your Electricity Board. It is usually 100 amps, but 80 amps or even 60 amps are sometimes found in older houses.

You then need to assess the current demand of the entire system, including the extra circuit, in order to check that the load capacity of the service cable is adequate. However, it is extremely unlikely that all the circuits in a house will be drawing power at the same time, so the I.E.E. wiring regulations suggest a formula for discounting part of the nominal load.

In the case of 30 amp power circuits, this means calculating the first 30 amp circuit at 100 per cent, and all others at 40 per cent. For 5 amp lighting circuits, all the loads are calculated at the same rate—66 per cent. In assessing the current demand of a cooker, the first 10 amp load is taken at 100 per cent and the remaining load at 30 per cent. Where the cooker control unit has a 13 amp socket outlet for a kettle, a load of 5 amps is added.

Fixed appliances with their own circuits, such as immersion heaters, are calculated at 100 per cent.

In the example below, the total current demand is 109.9 amps—exceeding the normal 100 amp rating of the Electricity Board's service fuse. A difference of, say, 1.5 amp may be ignored, but if the difference is as much as 10 amps, you should consult the Electricity Board. In such cases, it may be necessary to forego the extra circuit or to lay a new service cable with a larger capacity.

Calculating the Load on a System

Circuit	Formula	Result
5A lighting	66% of 5 amps	3.3 amps
5A lighting	66% of 5 amps	3.3 amps
5A lighting	66% of 5 amps	3.3 amps
30A power	100% of 30 amps	30.0 amps
30A power	40% of 30 amps	12.0 amps
30A power	40% of 30 amps	12.0 amps
30A power	40% of 30 amps	12.0 amps
30A cooker	100% of 10 amps 30% of 20 amps	10.0 amps 6.0 amps
13A cooker socket outlet	100% of 5 amps	5.0 amps
13A immersion heater	100% of 13 amps	13.0 amps
		109.9 amps

Safety Rules and Regulations

Safety measures are of paramount importance when you are working on electric wiring and appliances. Remember at all times that electricity is potentially dangerous. Your domestic mains supply can give an electric shock powerful enough to kill. And, with electricity, comes the risk of fire.

You are protected against shock and other hazards as long as you observe all the basic rules for safety:

□ Never tackle an electrical job unless it is within your capabilities.

□ Always unplug an appliance before working on it. Before working on fixed wiring always turn off the power at the mains, and remove the appropriate circuit fuses. Leave the fuses out until the work is completed; leave the switch off until the work is complete and the fuses replaced.

□ Never touch parts of the plumbing system or gas piping while working with electricity. Avoid standing in a damp environment, and never touch electrical equipment with wet hands.

□ Never run a flex beneath carpets or floor covering in places where there is the possibility of the flex being stepped on: it may become dangerously worn.

□ Never use ordinary staples to secure a flex along the top of a skirting board, or they may cut through the insulation and make contact with naked wires.

□ Always renew worn or damaged flex with new flex of the correct type. Never use insulation tape to join two pieces of flex or to cover up frayed flex.

□ All electrical fittings and accessories should be approved by one of the recognized authorities, such as the British Standards Institution, the Association of Short Circuit Testing Authorities (ASTA), the British Approvals Service for Electric Cable (BASEC) or the British Electrotechnical Approvals Board (BEAB). You should never use any items of equipment that are damaged or worn.

□ Never overload a circuit by adding more lights or socket outlets than it can take.

□ Never make the fundamental error of connecting a live wire to a neutral terminal or a neutral wire to a live terminal.

□ Never replace a blown fuse with one of a higher rating.

□ Never attempt to extend wiring so that it runs out of the house to provide light or power for a garage, greenhouse or swimming pool. Leave such work to a qualified electrician.

□ To ensure the long-term safety of electrical work, follow the standard procedures exactly—take no short cuts—and test the finished job carefully.

The Most Dangerous Room in the House

The proximity of electricity and water makes the bathroom or shower-room potentially the most hazardous room in the house. Bathrooms are, therefore, subject to very strict safety regulations:

□ It is against I.E.E. wiring regulations to install a socket outlet in a room containing a fixed bath or shower. The one exception is a purpose-made shaver-unit socket that complies with BS 3052 and incorporates an isolating transformer.

□ In general, all lights and appliances should be operated by switches or controls that are out of the reach of anyone using the bath or shower. A wall-mounted electric heater with exposed elements must always be sited out of reach. An exception to the general rule is a switch incorporated into an electric shower unit, but the unit must conform with BS 3456.

□ No wall switches for lights should be fitted in the bathroom. Lights must either be controlled by switches outside the room, or they must be operated by pull cords that are inside the room.

□ All lampholders must be fixed so as to be out of reach of anyone using the bath or shower. If within 2.5 metres of the bath or shower, a lampholder must be constructed of—or at least shrouded in—some insulating material.

□ Never bring into the bathroom an appliance—a hair-drier, for instance—that is being operated on mains voltage.

□ Where a shower cubicle is fitted into a room other than a bathroom, any existing socket outlet in that room must be at least 2.5 metres from the cubicle.

□ All electrical appliances with exposed conductive metal parts—a towel rail, for example—must be earthed and, at the same time, must be connected to accessible conductive parts of other equipment.

Stripping Flex and Cable

An electrical connection is made when the cable or flex that carries the current is wired up to the terminals in a switch, plug or socket. To prepare the wiring for such a connection, the end of the cable or flex must first be stripped of its sheath and the individual conductors of their insulating material. The exposed copper conductors can then be attached to the terminals.

You can use a utility knife to strip the wiring but do not use scissors or a knife to strip the conductors. Wire strippers *(page 89)* are safer as they are designed to do an accurate job. Since they can be set to the diameter of the flex or cable and individual conductors, they are less likely to nick the metal wire and cause an electrical hazard.

The sheath should be removed only from the cable or flex that will be contained by the plug or socket. As a precaution, leave about 10 mm of sheath inside the fitting. From the conductors themselves, strip away the minimum length of insulation—10 mm should be ample: exposed wires at the terminal could touch each other and cause a short circuit. Bared conductors in flex should be twisted tightly. For a screw terminal, bend them double and feed them through the hole in the terminal to give maximum contact between the wire and the terminal *(page 102)*. For a clamp terminal, wind the twisted wires round the shank. Cable conductors, which are solid, should be attached straight and not bent.

Before connecting the earth wire of a cable, slip insulating green and yellow sleeving over the conductor *(right below)*. Buy sleeving that matches the diameter of the conductor and cut it to length.

1 **Cutting the sheath.** Mark off on the sheath the length of the wire you need to expose. Using a sharp utility knife, slit along the length of the sheath, taking care not to cut into any of the insulated wires: if you do, cut through at the point of damage and begin again. Always hold the knife so that it points away from your body and your hands.

2 **Exposing the wires.** Peel the sheath back away from the wires. Bend it backwards so that it almost doubles up on itself. Slip the knife into the fold and cut the sheath. Again, be sure to cut away from your body.

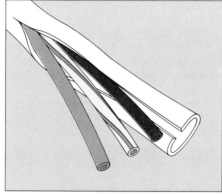

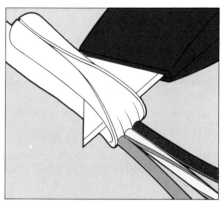

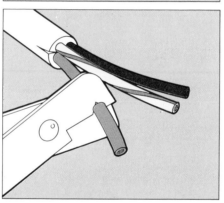

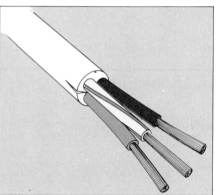

3 **Removing the insulation.** Set a pair of wire strippers to the diameter of the wire. Attach the wire strippers to one of the insulated cores and, twisting the tool back and forwards, remove the plastic. Remove an equal amount of insulation from the other wires.

4 **Preparing the wires.** With your fingers, twist together the exposed copper strands of each of the neutral, live and earth conductors so that each of the three cores is compact and separate from the others.

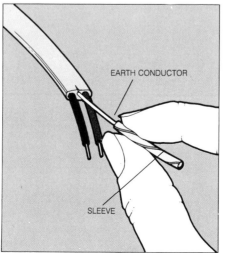

EARTH CONDUCTOR

SLEEVE

Insulating an Earth Wire

Sleeving the conductor. Most cables have bare earth wires, a hazard if the wire touches an exposed section of a live or neutral wire. Sleeve the earth conductor with insulating material of the appropriate diameter. Cut the insulating material slightly shorter than the length of the exposed earth conductor. Push and twist the sleeving on to the earth core *(left)*.

Changing a Plug Correctly and Efficiently

Wiring a plug to the flex of an appliance is the commonest of all electrical operations for most householders. If you have ring final circuits (pages 90–91), your plug will have three square (flat-sided) pins and contain its own cartridge fuse. With the older radial wiring you will have round-pin plugs—without integral fuses.

It is essential that each conductor in the flex should be connected to the correct terminal, according to the identifying colours of the insulation (page 95).

For all kinds of plugs, the method of wiring is essentially the same. The terminals may have pillar-type connectors, through which you thread the tip of the conductor before securing it with the screw, as in the demonstration below. With connectors of the clamp type (box, below), wind the tip clockwise round the shank and screw down the washer to clamp it.

The fuse in a square-pin plug acts for the single appliance as a circuit fuse does for the house wiring (page 93): if a fault results in an overcurrent, the fuse blows, breaks the circuit and prevents overheat-ing. It is vital to use the right fuse: 13 amp (a brown cartridge) for appliances between 720 and 3,000 watts, such as irons and kettles; 3 amp (red) for most appliances up to 720 watts, such as lights and radios.

Plugs are usually sold with a 13 amp fuse in place. Always check the rating of your appliance and change the fuse if necessary, otherwise the circuit will not be properly protected. With a 13 amp fuse in the plug, for example, a circuit fault could damage the flex of a hi-fi (rating perhaps 200 watts) long before blowing the fuse.

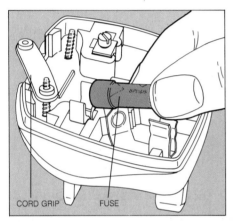

CORD GRIP   FUSE

1 Dismantling the plug. Undo the screw that holds the two halves of the plug together. Open the cord grip by undoing one screw and slackening the other. Remove the fuse from its holder; lever it out with the tip of a screwdriver.

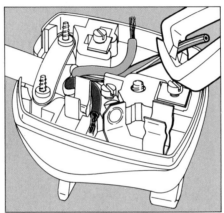

2 Preparing the conductors. Cut away 50 mm of the outer insulating sheath, and secure the flex under the cord grip. Trim the conductors to reach about 5 mm beyond each terminal. Using wire strippers, strip about 10 mm of the insulation from each conductor; twist the strands of wire to make a neat end and bend them double.

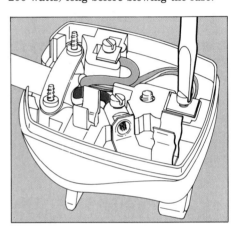

3 Securing the conductors. Loosen the screw of each terminal and feed the end of the appropriate conductor into the hole. Tighten the screw to secure the wire (above). Check that each conductor is secure and there are no loose strands of wire. Fit the correct fuse in the holder and replace the plug cover.

An Extra-Safe Plug

If you have an appliance that you know will be receiving hard wear—a power tool, for example, or a vacuum cleaner whose plug and flex may be jerked as the machine is moved around—you can buy a "safety plug" with a variety of special features. The type illustrated on the right has a screwless cord grip that is self-tightening when the flex is pulled. The pins of the plug are also insulated for half their length, so that even if the plug is not fully pushed home into its socket, or if it is accidentally half pulled out, there is little risk that someone will make contact with the exposed metal of the pins.

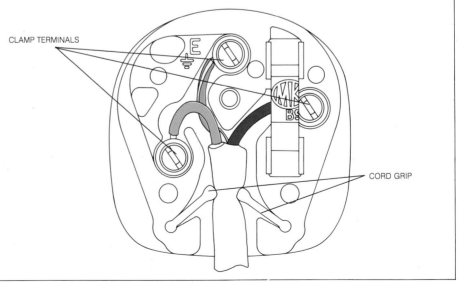

CLAMP TERMINALS

CORD GRIP

Extending the Range of a Flex

It is often useful to be able to join two pieces of flex, for example to extend the range of a portable appliance. There are several forms of connector to enable you to do the job safely and effectively.

Insulated fixed connectors *(below)* have cord grips and screw terminals similar to those inside plugs *(opposite page)*, with a screw-on cover so that the conductors are securely held and protected from being touched. Or you can choose an insulated plug-and-socket type of connector, which has pins on one half that plug into a socket on the other, so that the extended flex can be detached and put together again easily. The socket or female side must always be attached to the piece of flex that will plug into the mains, and the male side to the flex of the appliance. It is extremely dangerous to have the projecting pins on the mains side: when the plug on the other end of the flex is connected to the circuit, the exposed pins would be live. Both kinds of insulated flex connectors come in two ratings: the 5 amp connectors are suitable for small appliances such as table lamps, but you need 13 amp connectors with all appliances rated over 1,000 watts.

A third way of connecting flex is with a connector strip—a strip of plastic enclosing a metal interior; the plastic has holes for pairs of screws that may be screwed down to grip the ends of the conductors, making a connection between them by contacting a brass connecting rod within the plastic strip. Although plastic collars surround the heads of the screws they do not provide foolproof insulation, so the strip should only be used for connections that are not accessible to the touch—for example, inside the casing of an appliance such as a lamp base. Connector strips can be cut to one, two or three pairs of screws, to accommodate one, two or three-core flex.

Whichever kind of flex connector you choose to buy, you must make sure that the two flexes you are joining together match each other exactly in type: for example, use only two-core flex with two-core, three-core flex with three-core. Double-check that each conductor in one flex is connected to the like conductor in the other.

Before you buy and fit a flex connector, it is always worthwhile considering whether it would be more satisfactory to fix a new, longer flex to the appliance—or even install a new socket outlet if the appliance is in frequent use. In any case, do not trail a flex with a connector across passageways or under carpets or where exploring children could find it. There could be a risk of fire if the connector gets pulled apart.

Wiring a fixed insulated flex connector. Open the flex connector by unscrewing the plastic cover. Strip away the last 50 mm of the outer insulating sheath and secure the flex under the cord grips. Trim the conductors to fit and remove about 10 mm of the insulation from their tips. Fit each conductor of one flex into a pillar terminal in the same way as for a plug *(opposite)*, then connect each conductor of the second flex to the appropriate terminal on the other side: live must be connected with live, neutral with neutral and earth with earth. Tighten the screws on all the terminals and replace the plastic cover.

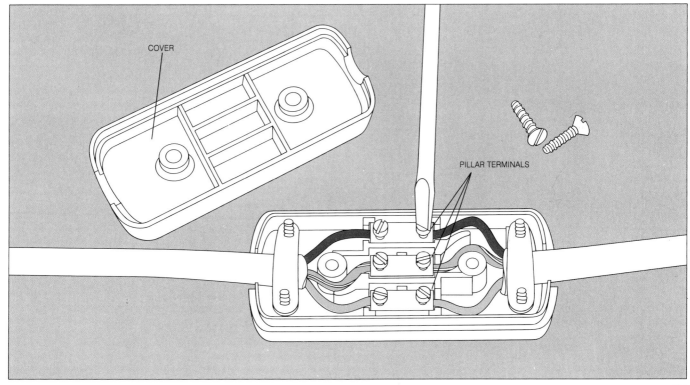

COVER

PILLAR TERMINALS

How to Rewire a Lamp

In spite of the great assortment of table lamp shapes and sizes, the electrical components and the way they are wired together are essentially the same. The chief constituents are: the lampholder, often with an integral switch; the base to which the lampholder is attached; the flex; and the plug.

A typical lampholder has three main parts: a screw-on top section; a middle section containing the contacts for the bulb and the terminals for the flex connection; and a bottom section which attaches the holder to the base, usually by means of a threaded stud or bush. If the lampholder has an integral on/off switch, it forms part of the middle section.

The lampholder may be made either of brass or of Bakelite plastic, or some similar non-conductive material. Metal and non-metal lampholders are very similar in their construction, but there is one important difference in the way they should be wired up: the metal type must be earthed to ensure against the possibility of a shock for the user (right), while the non-conductive fitting (opposite page) does not require an earth contact.

The two operations you are most likely to find necessary are replacing the lampholder—either because it is broken or because you want to substitute a modern, heat-resistant holder for an older metal type, as in the demonstration on these pages—and replacing a worn or too-short flex. If you are fitting a plastic lampholder in place of a metal one, you should cut off the redundant earth wire or, preferably, buy and fit a new, two-core flex of suitable length. You should also replace your flex if it is worn or the insulation is damaged.

An earthed metal lamp. This exploded view shows the components of a typical metal table lamp. A threaded ring (top) screws down to hold the wire ring at the bottom of the lampshade. The top section of the lampholder is attached by a second threaded ring that screws on to the bottom section, so that the switch and pin assembly is enclosed. The flex is led up from the lamp base (bottom) through a short length of conduit. The earth wire is screwed to a terminal in the holder, while the live and neutral wires are attached to the terminals beneath the switch.

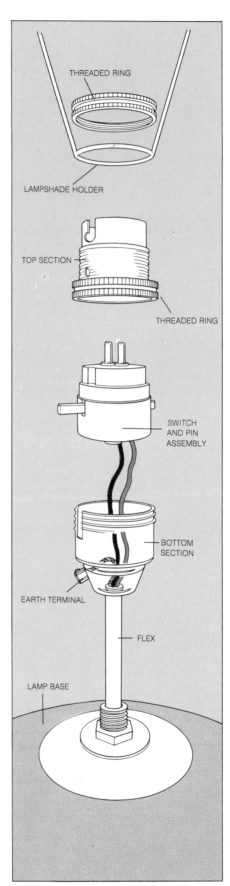

THREADED RING

LAMPSHADE HOLDER

TOP SECTION

THREADED RING

SWITCH AND PIN ASSEMBLY

BOTTOM SECTION

EARTH TERMINAL

FLEX

LAMP BASE

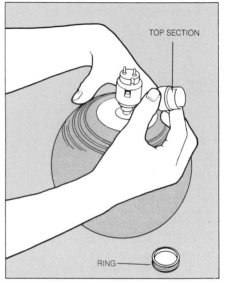

TOP SECTION

RING

1 Dismantling the lampholder. After removing the shade by unscrewing the threaded ring securing it, unscrew and remove the second ring that holds the top and bottom sections of the lampholder. Pull off the top section, revealing the switch and pin assembly.

Dealing with the Earth Wire

Cutting off the wire. Since the plastic fittings are non-conductive, they need no earth contact. If you are using three-core flex, snip off the green and yellow wire flush where it emerges from the insulating sheath (above). If you are replacing the flex, choose the two-core variety.

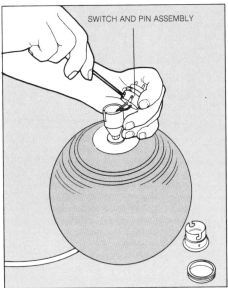

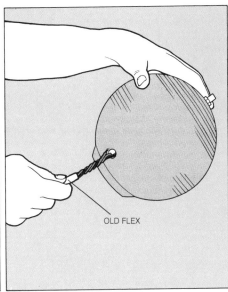

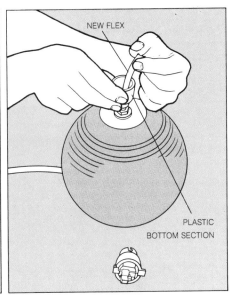

2 **Disconnecting the flex.** Unscrew the earth terminal—a small projection on the bottom section of the holder—and lift out the wired central section. Push up the flex a little from the bottom of the lamp to allow enough slack in the wires. Unscrew the terminals connected to the live and neutral wires until the wires are loose and can be drawn out. Unscrew and remove the bottom of the holder.

3 **Removing the old flex.** Pull the flex right out through the bottom of the lamp base. Push the new flex up through the lamp base until it emerges out of the top.

4 **Preparing the new flex.** Allowing enough flex to make the connection, fit the bottom of the replacement plastic lampholder over the flex *(above)* and screw it into place in the top of the lamp base. Strip off the outer insulating sheath from the end of the flex and prepare the tips of the wires by stripping about 10 mm of insulation, then twisting the ends tightly to neaten them and bending them double.

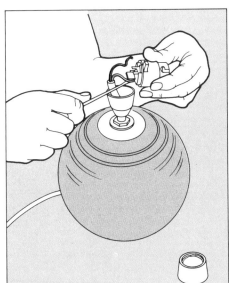

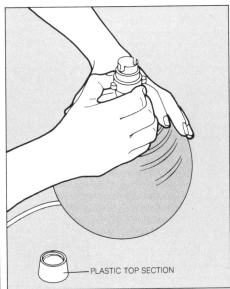

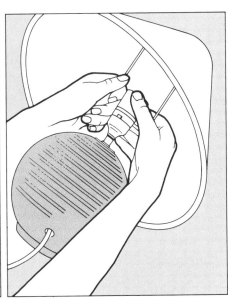

5 **Connecting the conductors.** Insert each of the live and neutral conductors into a terminal on the bottom of the switch and pin assembly of the new holder. Either wire may be connected to either terminal. Tighten the screws to the terminals to hold the wires firmly.

6 **Positioning the lampholder.** Pull the slack of the wires down by drawing on the flex at the base of the lamp, so that the switch and pin assembly settles into place. Turn or twist it down into the bottom section.

7 **Replacing the shade.** Fit the wire ring at the base of the lampshade frame over the lampholder, and screw on the top section to secure the lampshade in place. Do not overtighten the sections of the holder, or you may crack or distort them.

Replacing Wall and Ceiling Fittings

One of the easiest ways to transform the appearance of a room is to replace an outmoded light fitting with a new one. The replacement—on ceiling or wall—consists of three operations: removing the old fitting, wiring the new one, and then mounting it. The wiring is essentially the same for all fittings, though the procedure will vary according to the type of wiring system, either radial or loop-in. Before starting the job, turn off the power and remove the relevant circuit fuse.

There are two basic fittings: the pendant and the batten type. With a pendant fitting the lamp is suspended from a ceiling rose by a length of flex. Inside the rose are terminals for the flex and for the fixed mains wiring which enters the rose through a removable "knock-out hole" in the backplate. To accommodate loop-in fixed wiring systems, modern roses usually house three sets of terminals plus an earth. If you are wiring to a joint-box system you will use only two sets of terminals plus the earth; if you are wiring to a loop-in system you will use the three sets.

When you are replacing a ceiling rose, always renew the flex. If you are planning to fit a metal lampholder use three-core flex, which includes an earth conductor, and a ceiling rose with earth terminals.

A batten fitting comprises a lampholder and a base. Some have a base with an open back and three terminals, but most modern types have an enclosed base with backplate and three terminals plus an earth suitable for both radial and loop-in circuits.

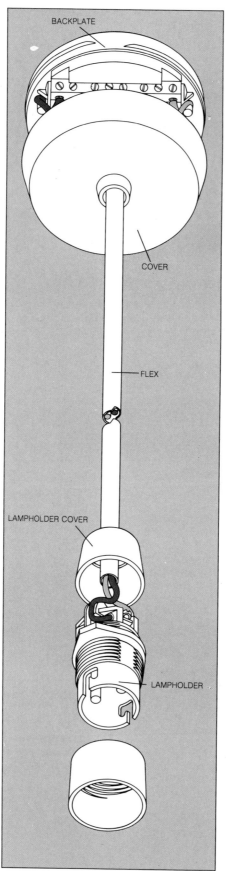

BACKPLATE

COVER

FLEX

LAMPHOLDER COVER

LAMPHOLDER

The classic pendant fitting. The lampholder hangs by flex which carries electricity from a ceiling rose to a lamp. When the fitting is assembled, the upper part of the flex is connected to a rose backplate which houses terminals for the fixed mains wiring in the ceiling as well as for the flex leading to the lampholder. The backplate has a cable entry knock-out hole for the fixed wiring. The screw-on cover has an exit hole for the flex. Most roses feature strain relief lugs, round which the cores of the lampholder flex are looped so as to prevent conductors from being pulled out of their terminals by the weight of the fitting.

The batten fitting. This type of fitting comprises two main pieces, a lampholder and a base that is screwed on to a ceiling or wall. The fixed mains wiring from the ceiling or wall is usually connected directly to terminals in the lampholder. To ensure that the terminals are safely enclosed, some bases, as here, feature a backplate. This model has three terminals plus an earth—sufficient connections for a loop-in system. Here the fitting is wired as for a joint-box system; thus the three terminals are not used.

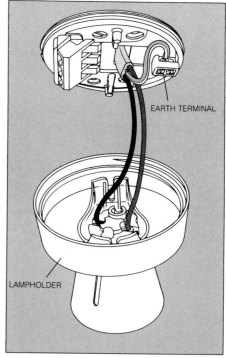

EARTH TERMINAL

LAMPHOLDER

Wiring a Pendant Assembly to a Joint-Box System

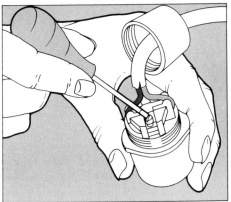

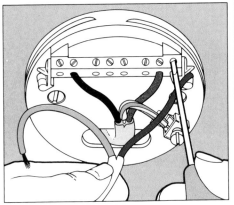

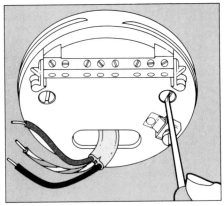

1 **Dismantling the old lampholder.** Switch off the power at the mains and withdraw the fuse. Unscrew the base of the lampholder from the cover; then, using a screwdriver, loosen the terminal screws *(above)*. When the flex is released from the terminals, slip off the cover and discard the old lampholder.

2 **Disconnecting the flex.** Unscrew the cover of the rose and slide it off the flex. Release the flex from the terminals *(above)* and discard it. Prepare new flex, stripping back insulation from the ends *(page 101)*.

3 **Removing the backplate.** Note where the red, black and green and yellow wires are fixed; release them from their terminals. Gather together the wires of the cable and straighten them. To remove the backplate, unscrew the two fixing screws *(above)*, then slip it free of the cable. Discard the old backplate.

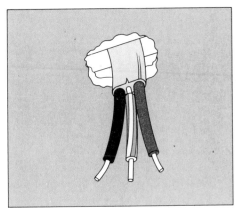

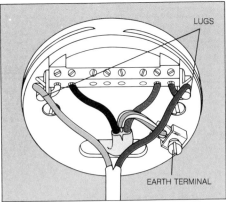

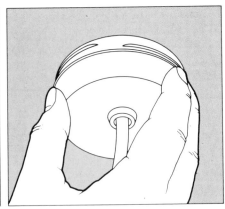

4 **Preparing the cable.** If the end of the mains cable is worn, pull out an additional 2.5 cm length of cable through the ceiling, and cut the same length from the end. Cut back the cable's outer insulating sheath and strip back 10 mm of insulation from each conductor *(page 101)*.

5 **Wiring the new backplate.** Feed the cable through a knock-out hole in the new ceiling rose backplate and fix the plate to the ceiling. Connect the fixed mains wiring *(Step 3)* and the new lampholder flex. Take the flex wires round the support lugs before connecting them.

6 **Placing the cover.** Slip the new rose cover over the flex and screw it by hand on to the backplate *(above)*. Feed the flex through the new lampholder cover and connect it to its terminals. Screw the parts of the lampholder together.

Wiring a Pendant Fitting to a Loop-in System

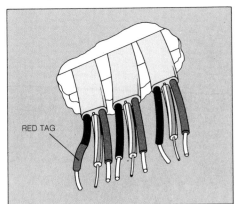

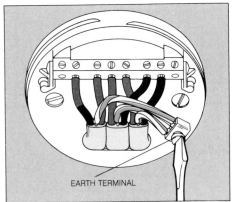

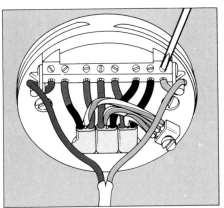

1 **Identifying cable.** Remove the old fitting *(Steps 1 to 4, above)*, noting from the mains wiring which blacks are paired and which is on its own; the latter should have a red sleeve or tag.

2 **Mounting the backplate.** Feed the cables through the backplate and screw the plate into position. Connect the fixed wiring as above.

3 **Securing the flex.** Wire up the new lampholder flex *(above)*. Connect the remaining parts of the fitting *(Step 6, above)*.

Installing Fluorescent Lighting

Although the initial cost of fittings and installation may be greater, fluorescent lighting not only gives more uniform illumination than incandescent lighting, but it can also lead to dramatic savings on energy consumption. A standard 40 watt fluorescent tube, for example, produces up to five times more light than a 40 watt incandescent bulb. In normal use, the same tube will also last about five times longer than the bulb—typically, 7,500 hours as compared with 1,500 hours.

There are drawbacks to fluorescents, however. The colour quality of the light does not exactly duplicate the "natural" effect of incandescents, though some types come very close. In addition, the design of the fittings is limited by the size and shape of the tubes, which are either straight, circular or U-shaped.

Fluorescent tubes operate on a principle quite different from that of incandescent bulbs. In the case of a bulb, the light is emitted by a tungsten filament which becomes hot and luminous when electric current passes through it. In the case of a tube, the light is emitted by an internal coating of fluorescent particles, which glow (or fluoresce) when current flows between two electrodes—one at each end of the tube.

To start the process, a surge of extra voltage is required. In the switchless or quick-start type of fluorescent tube *(opposite page, top)*, this is produced by a device known as a ballast. In the switch-start type *(oppostite page, centre)*, the extra voltage is produced by a ballast operating in conjunction with a starter switch.

Fluorescent fittings are easily connected to existing lighting points, although the method of installation will depend on whether your house has a radial or loop-in wiring system *(page 90)*. To find out which system you have, remove the cover of the ceiling rose. If only one cable is revealed, then you have a joint-box system and will need to follow the procedure shown on page 110. If two or three cables are revealed, then you have a loop-in system and it will be necessary to fix a joint-box above the ceiling, as shown on page 111.

A fluorescent fitting is usually simple to repair because its major components—tube, ballast and starter switch (where appropriate)—can be replaced without difficulty. The cause of most problems can be diagnosed by referring to the troubleshooting chart on page 111. If the cause is not obvious, you may still be able to diagnose it yourself by substituting new parts, one at a time. Be sure to use new parts of the same wattage and voltage capacity as those you are replacing. First replace the tube. If that does not solve the problem and the fitting is of the switch-start type, replace the starter switch.

Put in a new ballast, the most costly replacement, only as a last resort. If the ballast is faulty, you may find that it is only slightly more expensive to buy an entire new fluorescent fitting. To avoid making a mistake in wiring up a new ballast, transfer the wiring connections one at a time, checking against the diagram that is printed on the ballast.

Since most fluorescent fittings are made of metal, they need to be earthed. If your wiring is of an older type and has no earth wire in the cable you are connecting to the fitting, then it will be necessary to run a length of single-core PVC cable from the earth terminal in the consumer unit to the fitting. In this case, you should obtain the assistance of a qualified electrician.

A variety of tube colours. The quality of light produced by various fluorescent tubes is described in the chart on the right. Their colour characteristics—or colour renderings—are especially important if you want to match colours in a particular room, or if you need to know how well a particular tube blends with an incandescent bulb. Tubes classed as white and warm white are the most popular, and they produce the maximum amount of light per watt. Deluxe warm white tubes bring out certain colours with maximum intensity, but may produce up to 50 per cent less light per watt than other types.

A Colour Balance to Suit Your Purposes

Type	Colour characteristics
Northlight	Emphasizes blues and, to a lesser extent, greens. Does not blend well with incandescent light.
Daylight	Emphasizes yellows strongly and, to a lesser extent, greens; subdues reds. Does not blend well with incandescent light.
Natural	Emphasizes yellows and, to a lesser extent, greens and blues. Reds shift slightly towards orange.
Plus-white	Emphasizes yellows, oranges and greens; subdues deep reds. Blues shift towards violet. Blends well with incandescent light.
Deluxe natural	Equal emphasis given to blues, greens and yellows, but more to reds. Blends adequately with incandescent light.
White	Emphasizes yellows and, to a lesser extent, greens. Subdues reds and, to some extent, blues, which shift towards violet. Blends adequately with incandescent light.
Warm white	Emphasizes yellows and, to a lesser extent, greens. Reds slightly subdued. Subdues blues, which shift towards violet. Blends well with incandescent light.
Deluxe warm	Emphasizes yellows and, to a lesser extent, greens.
White	Subdues blues, which tend towards violet. Blends well with incandescent light.

Quick-start. Also known as switchless, the quick-start type of fluorescent lamp requires no starter switch and usually lights up without the few seconds' delay of the switch-start type. However, a quick-start may fail to live up to its name if it is turned on frequently and only for brief periods at a time. If problems occur, consult the trouble-shooting chart on page 111.

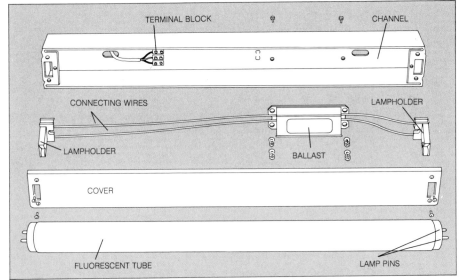

Switch-start. This type is the most popular fluorescent fitting for home use, and it consumes slightly less energy than the quick-start. It contains a starter switch, a small canister-shaped device which fits into a socket near one of the lampholders. To remove a worn-out switch, you simply press it inwards and then turn it anticlockwise. Press the new switch into the socket and turn it clockwise to secure it.

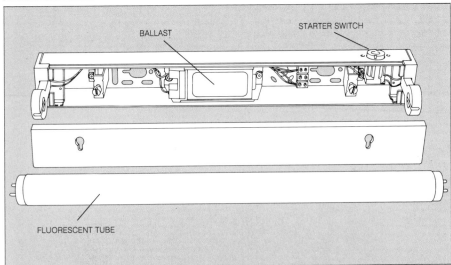

Miniature fluorescent. An alternative to the fluorescent tube is the so-called miniature, or compact fluorescent. It consists of two U-shaped fluorescent tubes inside a bulb and is fitted in the same way as an ordinary light. However, a miniature fluorescent uses only a quarter of the energy needed by an incandescent bulb of the same wattage, and lasts up to five times longer.

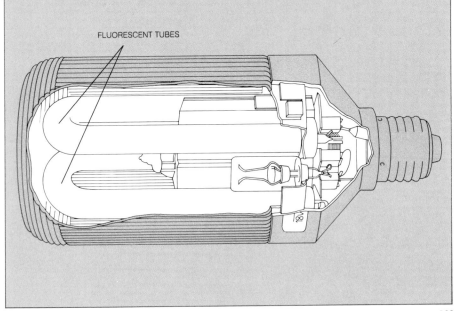

Mounting a Fluorescent Fitting

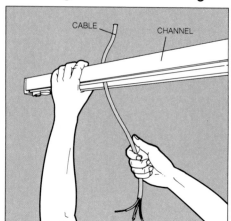

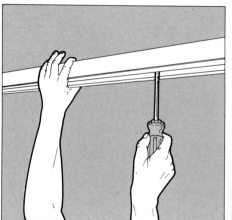

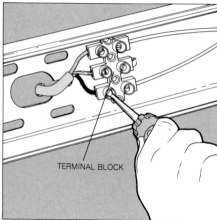

1 **Threading the cable.** Start by unscrewing the cover of the fluorescent lamp channel to gain access to the cable entry hole, the screw fixing holes and the terminal block. Then remove the ceiling rose and check the number of circuit cables. Where there is only one, thread it through the entry hole at the top of the lamp channel *(above)*. Where there is more than one, install a joint box *(opposite)*.

2 **Fixing the channel.** Having decided where you want to position the channel, hold it against the ceiling and use a gimlet to mark the fixing holes. These should penetrate through the plaster to the joists above. If you find that a fixing hole falls between two joists, then you will need to use plywood supports to span the gap *(page 113)*. Secure the channel to the ceiling using wood screws *(above)*.

3 **Connecting the cable wires.** If the cable from the ceiling is too long, use wire cutters to cut it to length. Then strip the cable as shown on page 101 and connect the wires to the terminal block on the underside of the channel *(above)*, fitting the red wire to L (live), the black wire to N (neutral) and the green and yellow wire to E (earth). The bare earth wire must be covered with a length of green and yellow PVC sleeving.

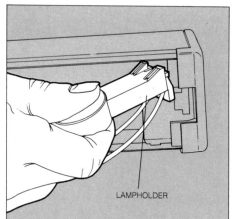

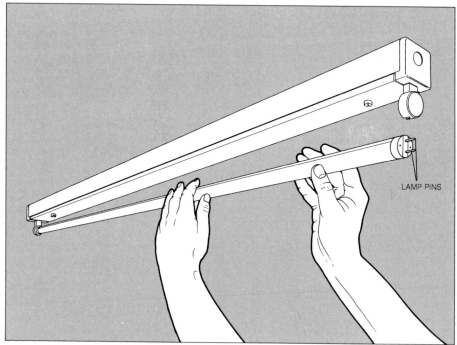

4 **Securing the lampholders.** In the typical domestic fitting, the tube is supported by a pair of pre-wired bi-pin lampholders mounted on detachable brackets. Insert each bracket into its appropriate housing at the end of the channel *(above)* and replace the cover.

5 **Fitting the tube.** Slot the first set of tube pins into the holder at one end of the channel *(above)*, then repeat for the second set. Twist the tube until it clicks into place. Make sure that the tube is held firmly in place before attempting to switch on.

Installing a Joint Box

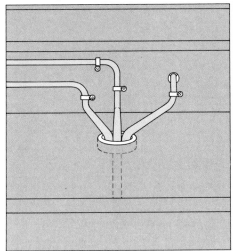

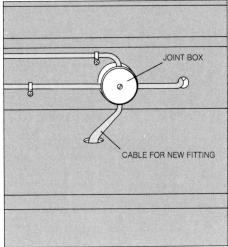

JOINT BOX

CABLE FOR NEW FITTING

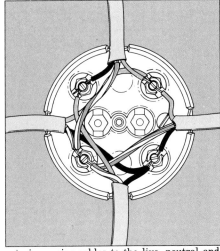

Fixing and wiring. A ceiling rose wired on the loop-in system usually contains the connections for three cables *(above, left)*. One cable runs from the previous rose, a second runs to the following rose and a third runs to the light switch. Where a fluorescent fitting is to be installed, remake the connections in a four-way joint box mounted above the ceiling *(above, centre)*, adding a fourth cable for the fitting itself. First, unscrew the ceiling rose and note where each wire is terminated before disconnecting the cables. Then lift the floorboards above *(page 119)* and screw the joint box to the nearest joist. To wire up the box *(above, right)*, connect both the incoming and outgoing mains cables to the live, neutral and earth terminals; the switch cable to the live, switch and earth terminals; and the additional cable to the switch, neutral and earth terminals. The additional cable can then be fed through the gap left by the ceiling rose and connected to the new fitting *(opposite page)*.

Troubleshooting Fluorescent Fixtures

Problem	Possible Causes	Solution
Tube will not light	Fuse blown or circuit breaker tripped	Replace fuse or reset circuit breaker.
	Tube worn out	Replace tube.
	Tube pins not making sufficient contact with lampholders	Rotate tube in holders.
	Incorrect tube for ballast	Check that tube wattage is same as that shown on ballast.
	Incorrectly wired ballast	Check wiring diagram on ballast. Rewire if necessary.
	Defective starter switch	Replace starter switch.
	Defective ballast	Replace ballast.
	Low voltage in circuit	Check leads from ballast. If necessary, get a contractor or Electricity Board to check house voltage.
	Air temperature below 10°C	Install low-temperature ballast.
Ends of tube glow but centre does not light	Defective starter	Replace starter.
	Incorrectly wired ballast	Check wiring diagram on ballast. Rewire if necessary.
	Inadequate earthing (common in quick-start type)	Check earth wire connections.
	Too high or too low a temperature	Ventilate fitting if temperature is too high. Screen or enclose fitting if temperature is too low.
Tube flickers or blinks	Common with new tube	Should improve with use—if not, replace starter.
	Tube pins not making sufficient contact with lampholders	Rotate tube in holders. If this fails to work, remove tube and check holders.
	Tube worn out	Replace tube.
	Air temperature below 10°C	Install low-temperature ballast.
Fixture hums or buzzes	Ballast wires loose or incorrectly attached	Tighten connections and check wiring against diagram on ballast.
	Incorrect ballast	Replace with ballast of correct type and wattage.
Brown or greyish bands about 50 mm from ends of tube	Normal	
Blackening at ends of tube	Tube worn out	Replace tube. If tube is new, replace starter instead.

Spot and Track Lighting Systems

A single light hanging from the centre of the ceiling may provide adequate illumination for a normal-sized room; but it is unlikely to show the room to its best advantage, and may even create an impression of dinginess and neglect.

Spotlights provide an alternative form of illumination which offers both practical and aesthetic advantages. Available with swivel brackets which can be adjusted as required, spots are particularly valuable in providing focused lighting for reading, sewing and other activities calling for close concentration. They can also be used to highlight particular features of a room, such as ornaments and plants.

There are four basic types of lamp used in spotlights: the general lighting service (GLS); the internally silvered lamp (ISL); the crown-silvered lamp (CSL); and the parobolic aluminized reflector (PAR) lamp.

GLS lamp. This is an ordinary tungsten filament light bulb and it must therefore be mounted in a reflective fitting. The beam of light emitted is broad and diffused, but up to 2 metres away from the subject a 60 watt lamp is sufficient for reading. Up to 1 metre away, a 60 to 100 watt lamp is sufficient for illuminating a desk or other working surface.

ISL lamp. Probably the most common spotlamp of all, this has a reflective coating of silver at the back which produces a strongly directional beam with a 35° spread. Used in the same way and at the same wattage as the GSL lamp, the ISL gives a higher level of illumination.

CSL lamp. This is silvered at the front so that light is thrown back to a reflector in the fitting. The result is a beam with a concentrated spread of about 15°, which is ideal for highlighting particular objects or areas—a wall hanging or a dining alcove, for example.

PAR lamp. Designed with a highly efficient rear reflector, the PAR lamp is available in two versions: one emits a narrow beam and is used as a spotlight; the other emits a wide beam and is used as a floodlight. Both versions of the lamp are available completely enclosed, suitable for use indoors or out.

Designed for mounting on walls or ceilings, most spot fittings have an open backplate which may be attached to a conduit box fixed over the lighting point. The box, which must be the same size as the backplate, has an entry hole for the circuit cable, an earth terminal for the circuit earth wire and two lugs for receiving the fixing screws. Since the box serves as a receptacle for the flex and cable connections, it must be made of a non-combustible material.

The installation of spotlight fittings can be greatly simplified if they are wired to existing lighting points, as shown on the opposite page. If, however, a ceiling rose reveals that the circuit is wired on the loop-in system, then it will be necessary to connect the spot fitting using the joint-box method described on page 110.

A main feature of spotlight fittings is their versatility: they can be fixed not only to walls and ceilings, but also to electrified lighting track. Originally developed for museum and shop displays, lighting track is now widely used in private homes because of the great flexibility it allows in the placing of spotlights.

A track is basically a strip of grooved aluminium, not unlike a double curtain rail, and because live, neutral and earth conductors run from one end to the other, spotlights can be moved to any position along the length of the track and aimed in almost any direction.

The track, which can be mounted on the wall or ceiling, has a cable entry hole and terminal block at one end for fixing over a lighting point. However, where the track is to replace an existing ceiling light (overleaf) and the circuit is of the loop-in variety, you will have to adopt the joint-box method of wiring referred to above.

Usually, track is only available in 1 to 3 metre lengths, but these can be clipped together with couplers—straight, T-shaped, X-shaped or right-angled—to form longer sections or different combinations.

Installing Spotlights

A single spotlight for the wall. In order to install the spot fitting, you must first remove the existing wall light. Usually, this will be mounted over a standard-sized conduit box sunk flush into the wall (below). Leave the box intact and use a two-way terminal block to connect the live (red) circuit wire of the cable to the live (brown) wire of the spotlight flex, and the neutral (black) circuit wire of the cable to the neutral (blue) wire of the spotlight flex. If the flex contains a green and yellow earth wire, connect it to the earth terminal in the conduit box. Position the spotlight base over the box and secure it with screws.

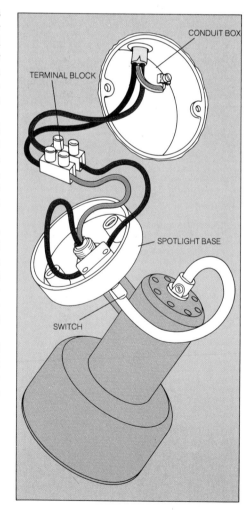

CONDUIT BOX

TERMINAL BLOCK

SPOTLIGHT BASE

SWITCH

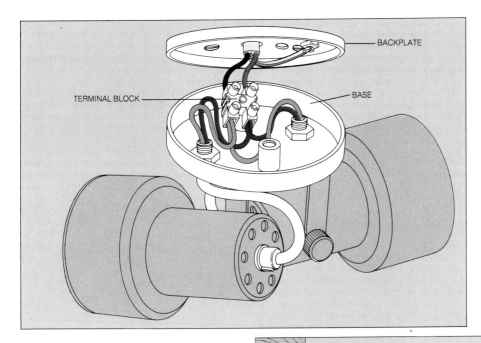

BACKPLATE

TERMINAL BLOCK

BASE

A double spotlight for the ceiling. After removing the existing light fitting and the ceiling rose, position the backplate on the ceiling. Push a gimlet through the screw holes in the backplate to make starting holes in the ceiling joist, then secure the backplate to the ceiling with wood screws. (If there is no joist immediately above the proposed site of the spotlights, install a plywood insert as directed below.) Connect the circuit cable and spotlight flex in the same way as for a wall-mounted spotlight *(opposite page)*, then secure the spotlight base to the backplate.

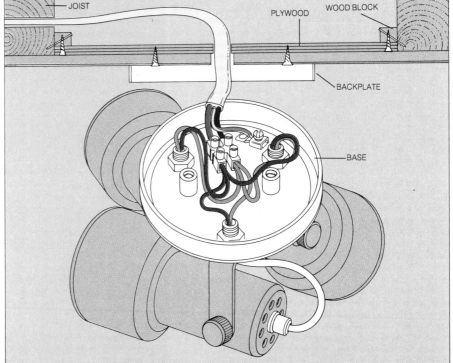

JOIST

PLYWOOD   WOOD BLOCK

BACKPLATE

BASE

Supporting a multiple spotlight. A multiple spotlight may be installed in exactly the same way as a double spotlight. If, however, there is no convenient joist or if the multiple fitting is too big to fix to a single joist, you will need to provide an alternative fixing base *(right)*. Lift the floorboards *(page 119)* directly above the fitting; cut a length of 50 mm thick plywood to fit between the two exposed joists, and screw two 50 by 100 mm wood blocks to each end. After drilling a 20 mm diameter hole for the circuit cable, place the wood against the ceiling. Feed the cable through the drilled hole. To hold the timber in position, nail the blocks to the joists, hammering the nails in at an angle so that they are firmly secured. Fix the backplate and spotlight base as described for the double spotlight unit.

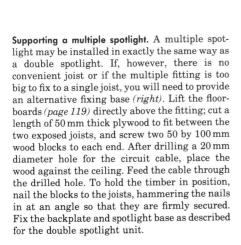

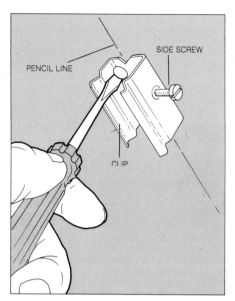

PENCIL LINE

SIDE SCREW

CLIP

Installing a Lighting Track

1 **Fixing the mounting clips.** Remove the existing light fitting and ceiling rose. Hold the track with the edge of its terminal block over the gap left by the rose and draw a pencil line on the ceiling along one side of the track. Position the first clip with its centre over the pencil line and mark the points where the fixing holes are in contact with the ceiling. Repeat for subsequent clips, spacing them out at regular intervals. Where the clips are positioned under joists, use a gimlet to make starter holes and attach the clips with wood screws; if the joists are not conveniently placed, you will need to use plywood supports *(page 113)*. Partially insert the side screws into the clips.

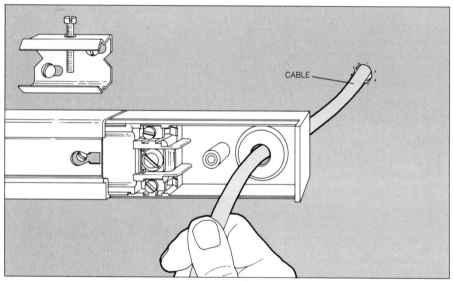

CABLE

2 **Feeding the cable.** First, make sure that the track is wide enough to cover the gap left by the ceiling rose. If it is not, plug the gap with plaster filler. Sand down the plaster until the surface is smooth. Unscrew the cover from the end of the track where the terminal block is housed and pull the cable through the hole *(left)*.

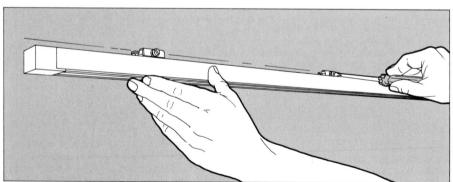

3 **Attaching the track.** Push the lighting track firmly into the mounting clips, feeding any excess cable back through the ceiling into the space between the joists. Tighten the side screws of the clips *(left)* to hold the track firmly in position.

4 **Connecting the track.** Attach the ceiling cable to the terminal block of the lighting track, fitting the red wire to the live terminal, the black wire to the neutral terminal and the green and yellow sleeved earth conductor *(page 101)* to the earth terminal. Check that the wires are firmly secured, then replace the terminal block cover plate on the end of the track.

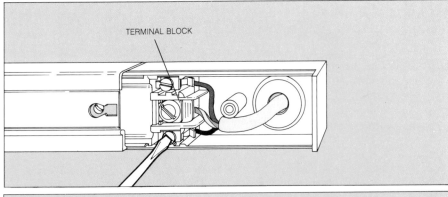

5 **Mounting the spotlights.** Open the adjustable arm of a spotlight fitting and slot the grooved end into the track channel *(right)*. Keeping the spotlight at an angle, move it into position and close the arm to lock the light into the track. Insert the remaining spotlights in the same way.

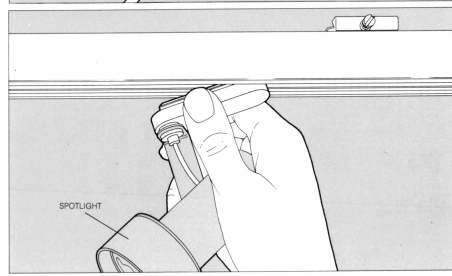

SPOTLIGHT

The Problem of Ceiling Roses

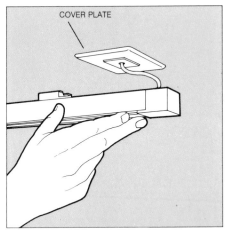

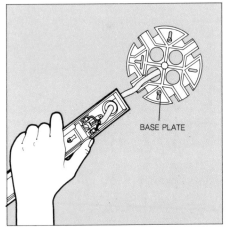

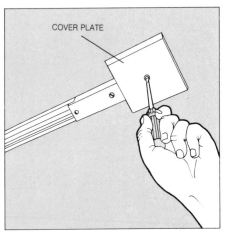

Fixing cover plates. Many manufacturers now supply plastic cover plates that enable you to install lighting track without needing to fill the gap left by the ceiling rose *(Step 2, opposite)*. In its simplest form, the cover plate is screwed to the ceiling with the cable exposed *(above)*.

A two-part cover plate. An alternative cover consists of two parts—a base plate and a cover plate—which are joined together to conceal the cable. With the base plate screwed to the ceiling *(above)*, the cable is connected to the terminal block of the track in the normal way. Any excess cable must be trimmed to length or pushed into the ceiling void. The cover plate is then screwed to the base plate *(above)*.

115

Replacing and Repositioning Light Switches

A light switch is always fixed in a flush or surface mounting box. The box is usually metal when embedded in the wall or ceiling, and has lugs which take the screws used to fix on the switchplate, and "knock-out holes"—removable discs—in the back and sides for cables. The red conductor carries current from the mains via a ceiling rose or joint box to the switch, and the black conductor takes the current on to the light bulb when the switch is in the "on" position. The wiring connections are made on the back of the switchplate, and thus completely contained within the box.

This basic arrangement holds any type of switch. Rocker switches with a seesaw movement are the commonest, having mostly replaced the old tumbler switches. Switchplates with up to three rocker switches are available. Ceiling switches used for safety in bathrooms (below, right) have a cord for control. A refinement of the on/off switch is the dimmer, with a rotating disc for adjusting the lighting level.

All these designs are reliable, and unlikely to develop electrical faults. But sometimes a switchplate cracks and you will need to replace it (below). You may also wish to substitute one sort of switch, such as a dimmer, for another (bottom, left). If you are installing a dimmer the maximum wattage must not be lower than the wattage of the light bulbs it controls.

Switch boxes can be mounted on the wall or sunk into the plaster. Flush switches are neater than surface ones, and safer because they are less likely to be knocked and damaged. The project opposite shows how to bury a box and cable in a solid wall.

Replacing a Switchplate

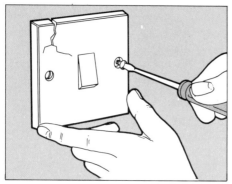

1 Unscrewing the switchplate. Turn off the power at the mains and pull out the fuse. Undo the screws that secure the switchplate to the box (above). Disconnect the red and the black wires from the switchplate but leave the earth wire connected to its terminal in the box.

2 Reconnecting the wires. Connect the red and the black wires to their terminals on the back of the new switchplate; these are usually marked L_1 and L_2 respectively. If the terminals are not marked, it does not matter which receives the red wire and which the black. The black wire is often tagged with red tape, as here, as a reminder that it is live whenever the switch is on. Screw the switchplate back into position.

Fitting a Dimmer Switch

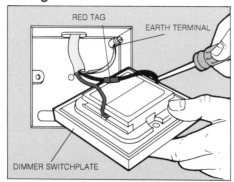

1 Connecting the wires. Turn off the power at the mains and pull out the fuse. Unscrew the existing switchplate. Disconnect the red and black wires from the switchplate but leave the earth wire connected to the terminal in the box. Reconnect the red and black wires to the appropriate terminals at the back of the new dimmer switchplate (above).

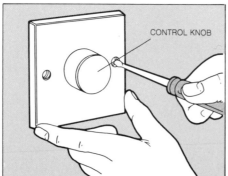

2 Fixing the new switchplate. Using an electrician's screwdriver, screw the dimmer's switchplate to the mounting box (above). (Dimmer switches are available to fit any existing mounting box.)

A Switch for Wet Places

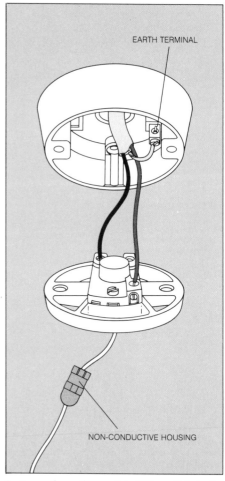

Anatomy of a ceiling switch. This switch is designed for the bathroom to prevent any possibility of wet hands coming into contact with live parts. It consists of a plastic base and a switch unit fixed to the ceiling and containing the usual three circuit wires. The light is turned on and off by pulling a cord which, for added safety, is of non-conducting material and generally in two lengths linked by a non-conductive housing.

Flush-Mounting a Switch

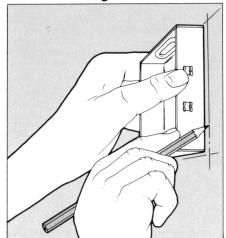

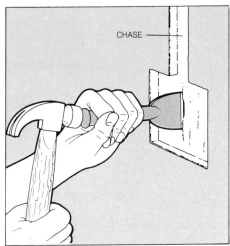

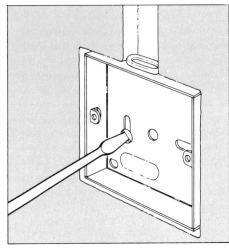

1 **Marking the outline.** Turn off the power at the mains and pull out the fuse. Unscrew the switchplate from the old surface-mounted box, disconnect the wires and unscrew the box. Hold the replacement metal box in a position the existing cable can reach, and use a spirit level to ensure its sides are vertical. Trace its outline.

2 **Knocking out the plaster.** If the cable is not already sunk, outline a 16 mm wide chase using the cable as a guide, then tie the cable to one side. With an electric drill, make holes along the outlines. With a bolster or cold chisel, chip out the plaster to a depth of 10 mm for the chase, and to the depth of the box.

3 **Fixing the box in place.** Place the box in its recess and mark on the wall the position of the screw holes at the back of the box. Remove the box, drill holes for the mounting screws and insert wall plugs. Secure the box in place with screws.

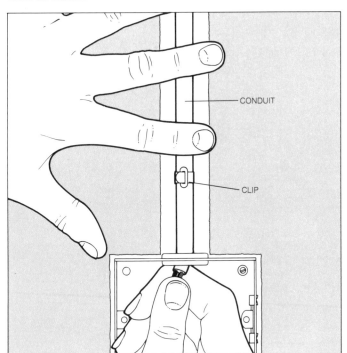

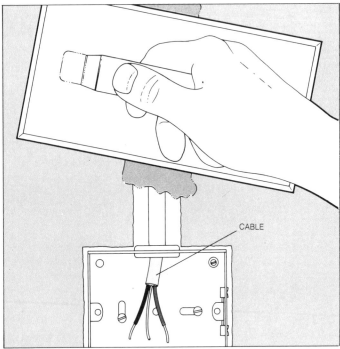

4 **Protecting the cable.** To protect the cable before it is plastered over, feed it into a 16 mm oval PVC conduit that is long enough to reach into the bush in the knock-out hole. Place the conduit in the chase and use cable clips spaced at 300 mm intervals to secure it to the wall until the plaster dries. Pull the end of the cable down into the box.

5 **Making good.** Plaster over the chase to just below surface level and smooth it with a trowel *(above)*. When the plaster has dried, bring the chase up to surface level with a cellulose filler. Smooth the surface with a wood block and fine sandpaper. Neaten the box surround with filler. Sleeve and connect the earth wire, then attach the switch-plate *(opposite page)*.

Installing a Two-Way Switch System

Lights that can be controlled from more than one point add greatly to the safety and convenience of your house. Indeed, two-way control is almost essential for stairs and for rooms with more than one entrance. The sequence on this page and opposite shows how you can add a second switch to control a light—a matter of running a special cable from the existing control point to the site of the new switch, and connecting the special cable to the one from the ceiling rose already feeding the original switch position.

The cable between the two switches is special in that it has an extra wire, which is necessary to complete the two-way circuit. Its colour scheme is quite different from that of the normal two-core plus earth cable. The insulated conductors are coloured red, yellow and blue. The earth wire is uninsulated, but should be sleeved with green and yellow plastic at terminations. The minimum size of three-core and earth cable to use is 1 mm².

For both the old and the new control positions, you will need switches especially designed for two-way switch systems, which have three, not two terminals on the back of the switchplate to accommodate the extra wire. (The earth wire connects to a terminal in the mounting box.)

The simplest job of installing a two-way switching system is in the sort of room shown here, with hollow walls and an attic above: the cable can be run without difficulty behind the walls and over the ceiling. Where the wall is solid, you will have to cut a chase in the wall *(page 117)* to hide the cable. For a ground-floor room, run the cable to the floor above; upstairs you will have to lift floorboards *(box, opposite page)* in order to route the cable across to where it must be lowered to the new switch position. If there is no access to the floorboards above (in a flat, for example), the best options are to route the cable under the floor or behind the skirting board, or simply to leave the cable exposed on the wall and ceiling. Never attempt to chase a ceiling, since it is very tricky to make good.

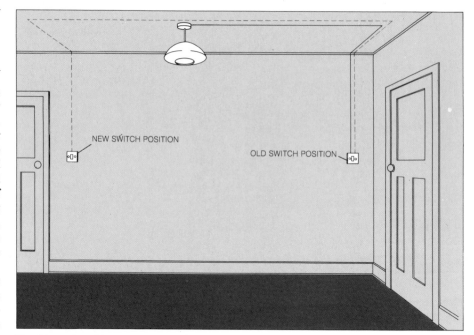

The wiring project. The aim is to install a two-way switch in a top-floor room at some distance from an existing switch. A new three-core and earth cable links the old switch position with the new: this runs to the attic, across its floor and down the hollow wall to the new switch position.

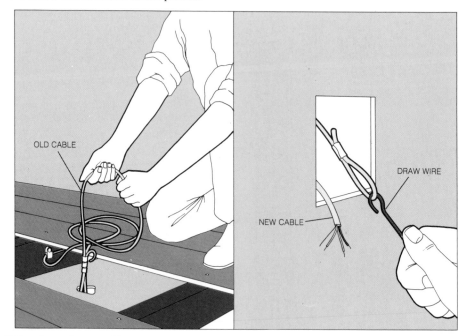

1 Drawing up the new cable. Turn off the power at the mains and withdraw the fuse. Unscrew the switchplate of the one-way switch, disconnect the wires and remove the box. Trim the end of the cable. Tape one end of the new three-core plus earth cable to the loose end of the old cable and hook a length of draw wire to the old and new cables. From the attic, pull the old cable up through the hole in the floor by which it descended into the room *(above, left)*. When the new cable appears, detach it and hook the draw wire to the old cable.

Draw up into the attic enough new cable to reach across the attic and down the wall to the new switch position, leaving the tail end of the new cable hanging out of the original switch hole ready to be connected to the new two-way switch. You can attach a weight to the tail end of the cable to prevent it from going astray behind the wall. At the downstairs switch hole, pull on the draw wire to bring the old cable back down for reconnection *(above, right)*.

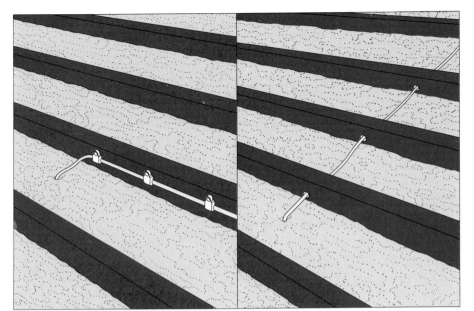

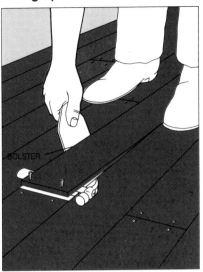

Lifting up the Floorboards

2 **Routing the cable.** Cut a hole for the cable in the wall in the new switch position and drill a hole in the attic directly above it. Run the new cable through the attic to the new hole. If the cable extends along the length of the joist, clip it to the side of the joist *(above, left)*; if it is routed across the joists, lay the cable over any insulation and bore a hole in each joist 50 mm from the top and bottom through which the cable can be passed *(above, right)*. To ensure that the cable, when lowered inside the hollow wall, reaches the second switch hole without going astray, fix any small heavy weight—known as a "mouse"—to a piece of string and tie that to the cable. Grab the "mouse" when it hangs level with the hole and draw out the cable.

To route a cable beneath the floorboards, first check they are not the tongue-and-groove sort by inserting a knife blade between two boards: if they are, the tongue of the joint will block the blade's progress. In this case it might be best to call in a carpenter to saw through the tongue interlocking the board with its neighbours. To lift a board that has been nailed down, find one close to the point of access not less than 150 mm from the wall. Insert a bolster chisel on one side of the board, about 75 mm from its end, and lever the board up. Work from the opposite side, too, to weaken the nail fixings. Repeat 75 mm from the other end. After raising one end of the board, slide the handle of a screwdriver or a hammer under the board until you are ready to prise the whole board up. If there is no ready-made cut in the board in the area where you want access, use a tenon saw to saw through the board across the nearest joist and lever the board up with a bolster chisel.

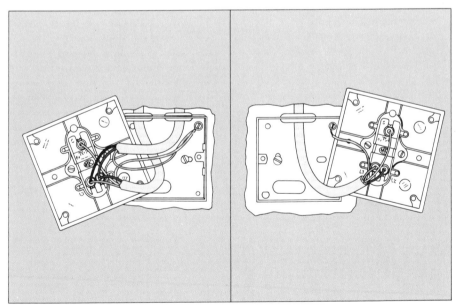

3 **Connecting the wires.** Punch an extra knock-out hole in the mounting box for the original switch position, add a bush, and pass both the old and the new cables into the box *(above, left)*. Fix the box back into the wall. Connect the wires to the switchplate: the original red (live) wire and the new red wire to the terminal marked L_2; the original black (switch) wire and new blue wire to the terminal marked L_1; and the new yellow wire to the terminal marked "common" or "C". Connect both earth wires to the terminal in the box. At the new switch position *(above, right)*, knock out the necessary cable hole in the second box, add a bush, pass the new cable through it, and fix the box to the wall. Connect the yellow wire to the "common" terminal on the switchplate, the blue wire to the terminal L_1 and the red to terminal L_2. Sleeve the earth wire *(page 101)* and connect it to the terminal in the box. Screw the switchplates to the boxes, replace the circuit fuse and turn on the power.

Selecting and Installing Single and Double Sockets

Wall sockets are the locations where the electrical appliances in a house are connected via their flex to the house's electricity supply. A socket is mounted on a box which may be either attached to the surface of the wall or sunk so that the socket is flush with the wall. Generally, sunken boxes are made of metal and surface boxes of white plastic. Metal surface-mounted boxes are often used in places such as garages where they are particularly vulnerable to knocks.

For the small portable appliances of the house, such as TV sets, electric fires and table lamps, the connection with the mains is made via a plug that is inserted into a compatible socket. Modern plugs are 13 amp and have square pins; the old-fashioned plugs of 2, 5 and 15 amps have round pins. On modern sockets the neutral and live holes are fitted with protective shutters to prevent fingers or screwdrivers from being poked inside. The shutters do not open until the long top pin makes contact with the earth terminal, thereby earthing the appliance before any contact is made with the live wires.

Fixed appliances such as central heating pumps and cooker hoods are usually connected to the electricity circuit by a fused connection unit. Fused units usually have a switch and sometimes a pilot light.

In a bathroom, the only socket allowed is a shaver supply unit with an isolating transformer. The socket is designed to accept only two-pin shaver plugs.

Often the neatest place to install sockets is fairly near the floor of a room, but old people and invalids may find higher sockets more convenient. Never allow a socket to be installed less than 150 mm above floor level, or less than 150 mm above the level of the work surface in the kitchen: if too low, sockets are dangerously vulnerable to kicks and knocks.

Any socket that is cracked or chipped should be replaced without delay. The procedure (opposite page) is simply to remove the damaged socket, disconnect the cables from the back of the socket, and reconnect them in the same positions on a new socket. Sockets that are on a ring final circuit or in an intermediate position on a radial circuit (page 90) will have two sets of cable inside them, one to bring the current and one to take it away. Sockets on a spur from a ring or at the end of a radial circuit will contain only one cable.

If your sockets are attached to surface-mounted boxes, one precaution you can take to prevent future damage is to mount them flush with the wall where they are much less likely to be banged. The procedure for preparing the wall is the same as for flush-mounting a light switch (page 167); follow the directions opposite for the disconnection and reconnection of the cables to their terminals in the socket. The metal socket box designed for flush fitting is usually 25 or 35 mm deep. The sockets for 35 mm boxes are deeper than those designed to fit 25 mm boxes. Use the shallower box if you want to cut away as little as possible of the wall material behind the plaster; use the deeper box with its slim socket for the neater appearance.

If you find that you do not have enough socket outlets for your needs, you may be tempted to use adapters by which more than one appliance can be fed from the same socket. These are useful as a temporary arrangement provided that they are fused and that the total wattage you take from any one socket is no more than 13 amps. If you exceed the limit, the adapter can overheat and start a fire. No adapter is a good long-term solution.

The only safe permanent solution to a socket shortage is to install more sockets. This ensures that you have enough capacity and that it is available where you want it. Any number of extra sockets can be installed within a ring or radial final circuit, provided you do not exceed the maximum area that can be covered by the circuit (page 90) an provided the maximum demand of all the appliances does not overload the circuit (page 99).

Installing a socket in a new position means laying new cable, a task that not every do-it-yourselfer wants to tackle. Unless you are experienced with cable, you would be wise to call in an electrician for this job. A more straightforward way of adding capacity is to replace an existing box for one socket with a box for two sockets, known as a two-gang box. This project (page 122) requires no skills beyond those taught already. You can replace a one-gang with a two-gang box anywhere on a circuit, whether ring or radial.

Replacing a Cracked Socket

1 **Unscrewing the socket.** Turn off the power at the mains and remove the appropriate circuit fuse. With a screwdriver, remove the mounting screws holding the damaged socket to its box.

2 **Loosening the terminals.** Disconnect the wires from their terminals on the back of the socket. If the socket is on a ring final circuit or in an intermediate position on a radial circuit, the box will contain two cable ends *(below)*, with the corresponding wires from the two cables twisted together. There is no need to untwist the wires.

DAMAGED SOCKET

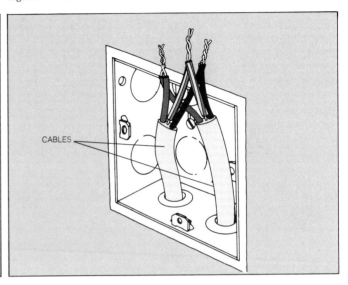

CABLES

3 **Reconnecting the cables.** On a new socket, reconnect the twisted wires to the same terminals as before. Screw the socket to the mounting box. Replace the fuse and turn the power back on.

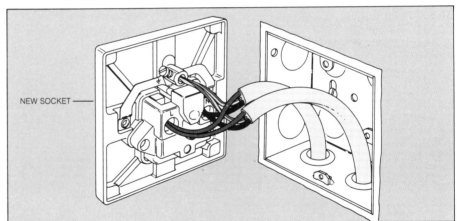

NEW SOCKET

A Single-Cable Socket

Connecting the cable. If, when you remove the socket *(Step 1, above)*, you find only one cable inside the box, it means that the socket is at the end of a radial circuit or on a spur from a ring. Disconnect the three wires from the old socket and reconnect them in the corresponding positions on the new socket.

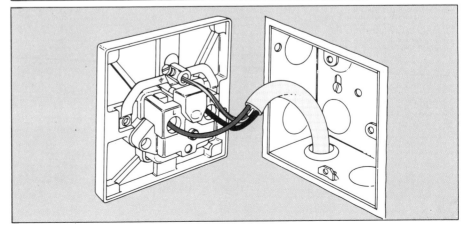

Replacing a Single with a Double Socket

1 **Removing the socket.** Switch off the power at the mains and remove the circuit fuse. Unscrew the one-gang socket from its box. If within the box you find two cables whose corresponding wires are twisted together, the socket is on a ring final circuit or in an intermediate position on a radial circuit. (For a box with only one cable, see opposite page, bottom.) Disconnect the pairs of matching wires from their terminals *(right)*.

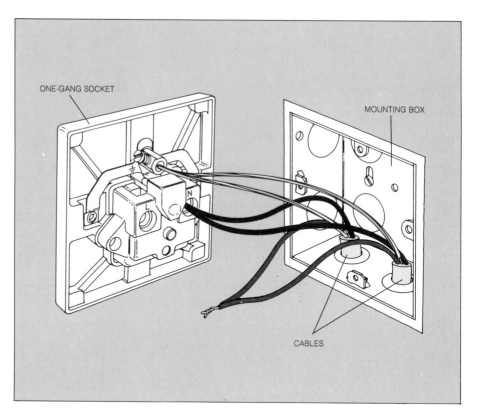

ONE-GANG SOCKET

MOUNTING BOX

CABLES

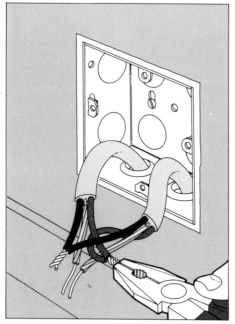

2 **Separating the cables.** Using pliers, untwist the bare ends of each pair of twisted wires *(above)* and disentangle the two cables. If the earth wires are entirely bare, sleeve them with green and yellow plastic *(page 101)*.

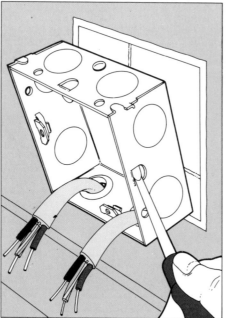

3 **Removing the box.** Undo the screws that fix the mounting box to the wall. If the box is flush-mounted in the wall, as here, prise it out with a screwdriver *(above)*. Remove the box from the wall, leaving the two cables protruding from the wall. To prepare the cables for entering the new, wider box, outline a chase in the wall and knock the plaster out to a depth of 10 mm *(page 117)*.

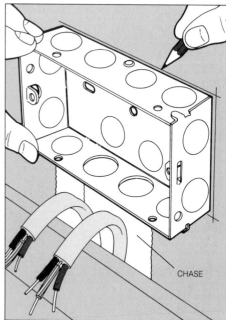

CHASE

4 **Marking out the new box position.** Centre the new two-gang box over the position of the old box, shifting it a little if necessary so that the cables are aligned with two of the cable entry spots in the box. Use a spirit level to check that the box's sides are vertical. Hold the box in place and draw round it with a pencil *(above)*. Remove the box and knock out the plaster and brick within the outline to the depth of the box.

5 **Fitting the new box.** Punch out the appropriate two holes in the new box for feeding in the cables and insert rubber bushes into the holes. Feed the cables up through the holes and fix the box in position in the wall *(above)*.

6 **Wiring the new terminals.** Twist together the exposed ends of the two live (red) wires. Twist together the exposed ends of the two neutral (black) wires. Twist together the exposed ends of the two earth wires. Screw the three pairs of wires into the three terminals marked respectively L, N, and E or ⏚ in the back of the socket.

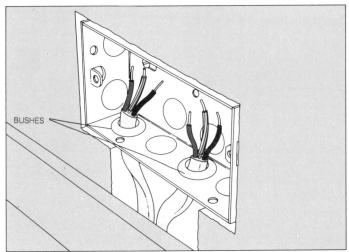

BUSHES

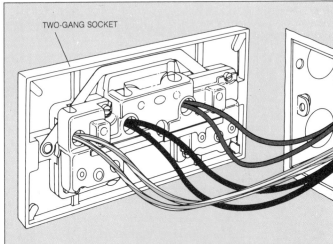

TWO-GANG SOCKET

7 **Fixing the socket.** Press the socket into position, taking care not to crush any of the wires. Screw on the socket. Replace the circuit fuse and switch the power on at the mains. If necessary, neaten the surface of the wall surrounding the new socket with cellulose filler.

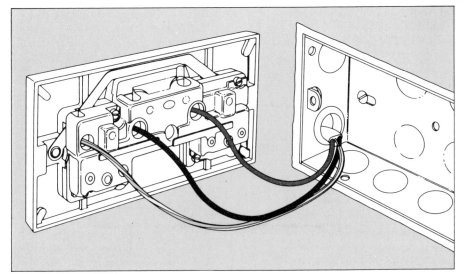

A Single-Cable Socket

Connecting the cable. If, when you unscrew the socket *(Step 1, opposite page)*, you find a single cable within the box, the socket is at the end of a radial circuit or on a spur from a ring final circuit. Disconnect the wires and remove the box. Sleeve the earth wire with green and yellow plastic if it is bare. Fit a new box *(Steps 4 and 5)*, punching just one hole for the cable to enter and inserting a rubber bush. Attach the red, black and green and yellow wires to the terminals on the back of the socket marked respectively L, N and E or ⏚. Screw the socket to the box.

Picture Credits

Sources for the illustrations in this book are shown below. Credits for pictures from left to right are separated by semi-colons, from top to bottom by dashes.

Cover: Martin Brigdale. 6: Ken Kay. 10, 11: Martin Brigdale. 12, 13: Drawings by Jackson Day Designs. 15, 16: Drawings by Peter McGinn. 17: Drawings by Jackson Day Designs – Drawings by Peter McGinn. 18: Drawings by Adolph E. Brotman. 19: Drawing by Adolph E. Brotman – Drawing by Adolph E. Brotman; Drawing by Jackson Day Designs. 20: Drawing by Adolph E. Brotman. 21 to 23: Drawings by Jackson Day De-signs. 24: Ken Kay. 26 to 31: Drawings by Jackson Day Designs. 32, 33: Drawings by Oxford Illustrators Ltd. 34, 35: Drawings by Jackson Day Designs. 36, 37: Drawings by Jim Silks. 38 to 44: Drawings by Jackson Day Designs. 45: Drawings by Jackson Day Designs – Drawings by Ray Skibinski. 47 to 49: Drawings by Ray Skibinski. 50: Ken Kay. 52: Drawing by Whitman Studio Inc. 53: Drawings by Whitman Studio Inc. – Drawings by Jackson Day De-signs. 54: Drawing by Ray Skibinski – Drawings by Jackson Day Designs. 55: Drawings by Jackson Day Designs. 56: Drawing by Jackson Day Designs – Drawings by Ray Skibinski. 57, 58: Drawings by Ray Skibinski. 59: Draw-ings by Ray Skibinski – Drawing by Jackson Day Designs. 60: Drawing by Adolph E. Brotman; Drawing by Jack-son Day Designs; Drawing by Adolph E. Brotman – Drawing by Adolph E. Brot-man. 61: Drawings by Adolph E. Brot-man. 62: Drawings by Whitman Studio Inc. 63: Drawings by Jackson Day De-signs. 64: Martin Brigdale. 66 to 83: Drawings by Jackson Day Designs. 84: Martin Brigdale. 88: Drawing by Oxford Illustrators Ltd. 89: Martin Brigdale. 90 to 123: Drawings by Oxford Illustrators Ltd.

Acknowledgements

The editors wish to thank the following: Barking-Grohe Limited, Barking, Essex; Bathroom and Shower Centre, London; British Ceramic Research Association Limited, Stoke-on-Trent, Staffordshire; Michael Brown, London; Building Centre, London; Alexandra Carlier, London; Sally Crawford, London; Delta Group plc, Birmingham; Denise Elphick, London; Erith College of Technology, Belvedere, Kent; Fraser Drury and Com-pany, Sutton, Surrey; Ernest Hall, Clac-ton-on-Sea, Essex; Hunter Plastic Indus-tries Limited, London; Institute of Plumbing, Hornchurch, Essex; Jacobs and Son Limited, London; Peter Kent, London; Key Terrain Limited, Maid-stone, Kent; Landis and Gyr Ltd., London; Jeremy Lawrence, London; Margot Levy, London; M.K. Electric Ltd., London; Dan McSherry, Camber-ley, Surrey; Marley Extrusions Limited, Maidstone, Kent; Deborah Martindale, London; Monument Tools Limited, London; Morphy Richards, Mexborough, Yorkshire; William Muncey, London; National Federation of Plumbing En-gineers, London; National Water Coun-cil, London; Judith Perle, London; Plas-tic Bath Manufacturers' Association, Glasgow; Ryness Electric Supplies Ltd., London; Sybille Safety Tools and Equip-ment Ltd., Heckfield, Hants; Tantofex Limited, East Grinstead, Sussex; Tenby Electrical Accessories Ltd., Birming-ham; Thames Water Authority, London; Stephanie Thompson, London; Vitreous Enamel Development Council Limited, Wadhurst, East Sussex; Wholesale Fit-tings plc, London; WYLEX, Manchester.

Index/Glossary

Metric Conversion Chart

Approximate equivalents—length

Millimetres to inches		Inches to millimetres	
1	1/32	1/32	1
2	1/16	1/16	2
3	1/8	1/8	3
4	5/32	3/16	5
5	3/16	1/4	6
6	1/4	5/16	8
7	9/32	3/8	10
8	5/16	7/16	11
9	11/32	1/2	13
10 (1cm)	3/8	9/16	14
11	7/16	5/8	16
12	15/32	11/16	17
13	1/2	3/4	19
14	9/16	13/16	21
15	19/32	7/8	22
16	5/8	15/16	24
17	11/16	1	25
18	23/32	2	51
19	3/4	3	76
20	25/32	4	102
25	1	5	127
30	13/16	6	152
40	19/16	7	178
50	115/16	8	203
60	23/8	9	229
70	23/4	10	254
80	31/8	11	279
90	39/16	12 (1ft)	305
100	315/16	13	330
200	77/8	14	356
300	1113/16	15	381
400	153/4	16	406
500	1911/16	17	432
600	235/8	18	457
700	279/16	19	483
800	311/2	20	508
900	357/16	24 (2ft)	610
1000 (1m)	393/8		

Metres to feet/inches		Yards to metres	
		1	0.914
2	6' 7"	2	1.83
3	9' 10"	3	2.74
4	13' 1"	4	3.65
5	16' 5"	5	4.57
6	19' 8"	6	5.49
7	23' 0"	7	6.40
8	26' 3"	8	7.32
9	29' 6"	9	8.23
10	32' 10"	10	9.14
20	65' 7"	20	18.29
50	164' 0"	50	45.72
100	328' 7"	100	91.44

Conversion factors

Length

1 millimetre (mm)	= 0.0394 in
1 centimetre (cm)/10 mm	= 0.3937 in
1 metre/100 cm	= 39.37 in/3.281 ft/1.094 yd
1 kilometre (km)/1000 metres	= 1093.6 yd/0.6214 mile
1 inch (in)	= 25.4 mm/2.54 cm
1 foot (ft)/12 in	= 304.8 mm/30.48 cm/0.3048 metre
1 yard (yd)/3 ft	= 914.4 mm/91.44 cm/0.9144 metre
1 mile/1760 yd	= 1609.344 metres/1.609 km

Area

1 square centimetre (sq cm)/ 100 square millimetres (sq mm)	= 0.155 sq in
1 square metre (sq metre)/10,000 sq cm	= 10.764 sq ft/1.196 sq yd
1 are/100 sq metres	= 119.60 sq yd/0.0247 acre
1 hectare (ha)/100 ares	= 2.471 acres/0.00386 sq mile
1 square inch (sq in)	= 645.16 sq mm/6.4516 sq cm
1 square foot (sq ft)/144 sq in	= 929.03 sq cm
1 square yard (sq yd)/9 sq ft	= 8361.3 sq cm/0.8361 sq metre
1 acre/4840 sq yd	= 4046.9 sq metres/0.4047 ha
1 square mile/640 acres	= 259 ha/2.59 sq km

Volume

1 cubic centimetre (cu cm)/ 1000 cubic millimetres (cu mm)	= 0.0610 cu in
1 cubic decimetre (cu dm)/1000 cu cm	= 61.024 cu in/0.0353 cu ft
1 cubic metre/1000 cu dm	= 35.3146 cu ft/1.308 cu yd
1 cu cm	= 1 millilitre (ml)
1 cu dm	= 1 litre see **Capacity**
1 cubic inch (cu in)	= 16.3871 cu cm
1 cubic foot (cu ft)/1728 cu in	= 28.3168 cu cm/0·0283 cu metre
1 cubic yard (cu yd)/27 cu ft	= 0.7646 cu metre

Capacity

1 litre	= 1.7598 pt/0.8799 qt/0.22 gal
1 pint (pt)	= 0.568 litre
1 quart (qt)	= 1.137 litres
1 gallon (gal)	= 4.546 litres

Weight

1 gram (g)	= 0.035 oz
1 kilogram (kg)/1000 g	= 2.20 lb/35.2 oz
1 tonne/1000 kg	= 2204.6 lb/0.9842 ton
1 ounce (oz)	= 28.35 g
1 pound (lb)	= 0.4536 kg
1 ton	= 1016 kg

Pressure

1 gram per square metre (g/metre^2)	= 0.0292 oz/sq yd
1 gram per square centimetre (g/cm^2)	= 0.226 oz/sq in
1 kilogram per square centimetre (kg/cm^2)	= 14.226 lb/sq in
1 kilogram per square metre (kg/metre^2)	= 0.205 lb/sq ft
1 pound per square foot (lb/ft^2)	= 4.882 kg/metre^2
1 pound per square inch (lb/in^2)	= 703.07 kg/metre^2
1 ounce per square yard (oz/yd^2)	= 33.91 g/metre^2
1 ounce per square foot (oz/ft^2)	= 305.15 g/metre^2

Temperature

To convert °F to °C, subtract 32, then divide by 9 and multiply by 5
To convert °C to °F, divide by 5 and multiply by 9, then add 32

Phototypeset by Tradespools Limited, Frome, Somerset
Printed and bound by Artes Gráficas, Toledo, SA, Spain
D. L. TO: 173 -1984